Seeking Balance in an Unbalanced World

• • •

A TEACHER'S JOURNEY

SEEKING
BALANCE IN AN
UNBALANCED
WORLD

A TEACHER'S JOURNEY

. . .

Angela Schmidt Fishbaugh

Redleaf Press®
www.redleafpress.org
800-423-8309

b 31529616

Published by Redleaf Press
10 Yorkton Court
St. Paul, MN 55117
www.redleafpress.org

Text excerpt on page 131 from *A Better Way to Live* by Og Mandino, copyright 1990 by Og Mandino. New York: Bantam Books, 1990. Reprinted with permission from Bantam Books, a division of Random House, Inc.

First edition 2009
Developmental edit by Jean Cook
Cover design by Soulo
Interior typeset in Minion Pro and designed by Ann Sudmeier
Interior photos courtesy of the author
Photo on page 48 by Lois Deming
Printed in the United States of America
15 14 13 12 11 10 09 08   1 2 3 4 5 6 7 8

Library of Congress Cataloging-in-Publication Data
Fishbaugh, Angela Schmidt.
    Seeking balance in an unbalanced world : a teacher's journey /
  Angela Schmidt Fishbaugh. — 1st ed.
      p.   cm.
    ISBN 978-1-933653-69-3
    1. Reflective teaching.   2. Motivation in education.   I. Title.
  LB1025.3.F57 2009
  371.102—dc22

                                          2008021079

Printed on 100 percent postconsumer waste paper

371.102
.F57
2009

FSC
Recycled
Supporting responsible
use of forest resources
Cert no. SW-COC-002283
www.fsc.org
© 1996 Forest Stewardship Council

This book is dedicated to everyone
who ever encouraged me to shine . . .
you know who you are!

Seeking Balance in an Unbalanced World

Acknowledgments

To my parents, for giving me everything you had during your short time on this earth,

To my children, for helping me celebrate life and model daily balance,

To my husband, for all your wisdom,

To all my family, brothers and sister, my dear aunts and favorite cousins, and my godmother, for everything we have been through together and your priceless humor,

To my dear friends, old and new, for enriching my life with your time and talks,

To my best friends at work, the colleagues I spend many of my waking hours with, for making it all so enjoyable,

To my past and present students, for all your pictures of you and me under the sunshine together, for your morning hugs and "I love you, Mrs. Fishbaugh!" words,

I say,

"Thank you for being with me on this journey!
I love you!"

Special Thanks

To my editor, Kyra Ostendorf, for all your time, dedication, and thoughtfulness. A special thank-you for your amazing encouragement. To Jean Cook, for your thorough work and support as well. To David Heath, for your direction and ability to connect (must be all those years of professional acting). To JoAnne Voltz, Eric Johnson, Laura Maki, and all the experts at Redleaf Press who helped make this piece glisten. You are all truly stars!

To my sponsor teachers, Christine Huggler-Wyant and Peg Patterson, for opening your hearts and classrooms to me.

Introduction

Never doubt that a small group of thoughtful, committed citizens can change the world. Indeed, it is the only thing that ever has.

—Margaret Mead, 1901–78, American anthropologist, author

I never thought I would experience having students throw chairs, curse, bite, and pitch conniptions so intense that I was not quite sure whether an alien might burst from their tantruming bodies. And I certainly never thought I would eventually think of such experiences as blessings. Today, I recognize that all those great efforts and struggles guided me down the right path. The challenging students, the demanding parents—and fortunately, the messages from those I worked with who said, "Angela, you are a great educator"—all added up over my years of teaching. With difficult children usually follow difficult parents, and I began to notice that each difficult student and parent who came my way were gifts. They were gifts because each one gave me a new strategy to put into my teaching toolbox. This book is a compilation of my tools. It includes the rituals I use to remain balanced during hectic and frenzied times. It is a repertoire of all my balance-filled ideas. It is for anyone who wants to be a well-adjusted teacher and human being.

Seeking Balance in an Unbalanced World: A Teacher's Journey is for teachers, parents, and students studying to be educators. It is for anyone who works in a school organization and wants to live a less chaotic life. This book is for those who desire to be fine role models in this now-unbalanced world of ours, especially those who work closely with our next generation.

Somewhere along the timeline of my life, I went from being a high-powered college student to a frazzled first-year teacher to a teacher handling hectic changes through a few different grade levels to a balanced human being. This is how I label myself now, and it is where I continue to develop and grow. When anyone asks me these days, "What do you do?" I always say, "I am a teacher." I know people automatically envision a public school teacher or someone who teaches others, but I remind myself that first I am a teacher of how to be a balanced person.

At some point through the years, I did not panic when each challenging child came through my classroom door. I did not panic. I actually began trusting that I had the right tools in the toolbox. I learned to trust the process. I learned to trust myself (which is also a gift). I became conscious of my own personal talents. I also became aware that everyone has personalized talents, and I was ready, willing, and able to use mine. I am now eager to work on anything that is put in my path.

The students have entered my classroom one by one with their challenges. In my early days of teaching, the students were considered simply delayed in an area or as having a young developmental age. In the early 1990s, I noticed that many students coming to school needed some speech improvements. In this day and age, many students are entering school who seemingly have never shared in a conversation with an adult. The challenging students are now entering school not quite knowing how to simply talk with someone. Today more and more students are arriving carrying serious issues. They come from foster homes because both parents are in jail for selling drugs, or they live with their stepgrandmother because their father died of a drug overdose and their mom is immersed in her own addictions. The issues are so deep and extreme that I believe teachers are not compensated enough to cope with the stresses that come along with these children, let alone trained to deal with any of these concerns. We as teachers have not only become health care workers, we are now to act as the children's parents and counselors as well. Today's teachers are overworked by the latest and newest curriculum they need to learn, worn out by the serious emotional issues that children carry to school each day, and underpaid considering the length and cost of our college education. Ask any teacher to share honestly about these issues, and you would realize we could form our own twelve-step anonymous group about the powerlessness we sometimes feel in this profession.

Children who are barely school age have full individualized education programs (IEPs) already in place. It bothers me as a teacher and a therapist that too many youngsters are carrying such heavy classifications today. Students are not simply considered developmentally delayed anymore. They are burdened with such labels as emotionally disturbed (ED); Asperger's, which falls under the autism spectrum disorders (ASDs) umbrella; or the classification that is lately being bombarded on our children, bipolar disorder. Of course, the old identifications continue as well. We teach children who have been diagnosed with attention deficit disorder (ADD), attention-deficit/hyperactivity disorder (ADHD), obsessive-compulsive disorder (OCD), and post-traumatic stress disorder (PTSD), all of whom are overactive and need excessive amounts of attention in our classrooms as well.

So, there you have it. The regular education teacher does not receive much training to work with these children. There is not a lot of money available to send us to be trained. There is a great deal of work to do and less help in the classroom. This is not a bad dream. This is reality. This is the reality in all public schools across the United States.

This was my reality only a few years ago. Instead of running the other way and choosing another path for myself, I chose to stay and make it better. Many days I thought the job was too much. It was borderline unbearable. I cried to my husband at night, and I was irritable to my family because I had depleted myself at school. I gave everything I had to the children in my classroom and their families. I basically had nothing left to give my family, let alone myself. This was my turning point. I realized I could not change others; however, I learned I could change myself. I turned inward. At this point, I was doing work in psychodrama therapy, which in simple terms is a role-playing and action-based therapeutic technique, and I decided to become a therapist as well. I also created and developed what I coined an individualized therapeutic plan (ITP) for myself. Quite similar to students' IEPs, an ITP looks at things from a holistic perspective. An ITP looks at all the dimensions of the self and includes specific ideas for those aspects that need to become more balanced in one's life. I truly believe it would be most beneficial, in terms of balance, if we teachers today created our own ITPs to help in preventing burnout.

My ITP looked at those dimensions of my life—my spiritual, emotional, physical, social, intellectual, and occupational aspects—and noticed that the largest slice of the pie was my occupational self. I had allowed my teaching career to swallow up the other important areas of my life. In my ITP, for my physical dimension I included that I needed to exercise four times a week for thirty minutes each time. For my spiritual aspect, I determined that I needed to do yoga for myself three times a week. My social dimension needed to visit with friends daily, even if it was only for five minutes. I made these and other changes until I felt balanced once again. I looked inside at what needed to change. I decided to live and teach by example, share by example, and basically do most things by simply being a balanced human being who cares. The entire world knows we need teachers who care. I want to be one of them. I was determined not to run away from the problems.

Rather, I chose to stay on my teaching path and offer my wisdom to others. This is how my book came about. My message is that you should trust your inner guidance system. Have faith and believe. Trust the life process. My path led me to share my talents. In fact, everyone's path is supposed to lead them to sharing their gifts with others. This book is my gift to the *deeper* world of teaching. Enjoy!

1

Become a Mindful Teacher

It is never too late to be what you might have been.
—George Eliot (Mary Ann Evans), 1819–80, English novelist

When I tell people that I am a teacher, I know many of them automatically envision a public school teacher or something similar, but the word *teacher* embraces a deeper meaning in my spirit. In my heart, I know I am here for a greater purpose. We are all here for a greater purpose. Knowing who you are and what your talents are will help you define your true purpose more clearly. My talent is about balance, and I know my purpose is to teach others about how to live a more balanced and fulfilling life. Balance to me means the opposite of compulsion. It is about being well rounded, open, and familiar with the whole self. It is about responding to life with your wisdom. A balanced person knows deeply what her spirit, mind, and body need to shine in this world, and then she applies it. This defines a well-adjusted being.

Shaping your values and becoming more of who you genuinely are as you continue on your journey are essential elements to being a well-rounded, balanced individual. Knowing who you are, becoming mindful of your authentic self, is a skill. It sounds simple, but in today's busy world we are playing so many roles and juggling too many priorities, so knowing who we are on this earth can be difficult, yet it is critical. It is critical because the world is starving for wise men and women. We already have enough chaos. The universe is hungry for your uniqueness. It needs your deep wisdom to shine on it.

Think about why you are reading this book. Perhaps you believe, as I do, that a great deal of your surrounding world is chaotic. I know I would like to see more balanced, peaceful individuals in this world. You, too, would like to be one of those well-rounded, wise individuals everyone wants to be around. Or perhaps you would like a little of the peace of mind you hear people talk about time and time again. Regardless of why you believe it is important to be balanced and teach balance, the world is hungry for these types of people.

So, how do you, as a responsible, functional person, become more balanced? How do you ensure quality time with your family with all the grocery shopping, laundry, cooking, cleaning, bills, appointments, schedules, and meals together? How do your nourish yourself to become a well-adjusted, balanced person despite all the demands from work, some difficult people in your life, the craziness of the media, and a world around you that is not rational or balanced itself?

First, you must understand the dimensions of the self. There are six dimensions to each individual. All of these dimensions need to be developed and balanced. In this chapter we will discuss exactly what makes up the self. We will learn about all the aspects that make up the whole self. We will define more clearly who we are and outline the steps we can take to become more balanced individuals. By simply being a balanced person, you are already teaching the fundamentals of balance to others. You are doing it by example, and people sense balance. It is important to note that we are multifaceted people and that each facet needs to be carefully examined. As we work on each part of ourselves, that area becomes clear. It glistens and eventually becomes so finely polished that it reflects your shine. Then you move on to the next facet. You will look at it and do the same enhancement, continuing on to each facet, polishing and developing it, enhancing and balancing each aspect as you continue on your life journey.

Stop for a moment to think of three pleasant individuals you know. I would bet the enjoyable individuals you name are working for the most part from a balanced state of being. They know, consciously or not, that they need to be secure in all areas. They are the people we enjoy being around. They are people we aspire to be more like. They share many characteristics. They tend to be friendly, outgoing, spiritually uplifting, and confident. They are smart, everyone at work seems to like them, and overall they are happy with themselves. Notice that I did not say they are perfect. They have days when they are off balance as well. For the most part, though, they've got it going. These types of people hold the secret to being balanced. Their whole self is balanced. Knowing all about your whole self is vital to being a well-balanced individual.

● ● ●

The Whole Self

I did not always know who I truly was. It has taken me many years to uncover what I do know of myself. Furthermore, I am still learning about the real me.

When I attended college in the early 1990s as a nontraditional student, I noticed that many other nontraditional students, such as those who served in the military and older students, succeeded at becoming exempt from a class called "Design for Active Living." I believe the college's philosophy was that the students who were older had life experience, which would be close enough to equivalent, so they were excused from the course. I am thankful I was not released from taking the course. Back then, my energy went toward taking care of my eight-month-old son and holding two part-time jobs, one as a waitress, the other as a bartender, while I attended college. Diving into any course about a design for living seemed quite appropriate for me at the time.

So I took the class, which was taught by a petite older woman known for her liberal values and lifestyle. She had an extremely kind heart and was always available to touch base. In this class I attained the knowledge that would later on help me in life. There I learned about the six dimensions that make up the whole self. Those ideas were originally developed by Dr. Bill Hettler and the National Wellness Institute in the Six Dimensional Model of Wellness that was created in the 1970s. Dr. Hettler is also the cofounder and president of the board of directors of the institute, based in Stevens Point, Wisconsin, whose mission is to serve those individuals and organizations that promote the best possible health and wellness for everyone. Essentially a person applies this holistic model of wellness to begin to see how the six dimensions of self—spiritual, emotional, physical, social, intellectual, and occupational—are interconnected and contribute to healthy living. The course I took did not offer detailed information about it but rather only summarized the basic ideas in one or two particular classes. Nevertheless, I ran with what was given to me. The ideas touched me so profoundly that the core of my spirit was put on an entirely different path. I am tremendously thankful for Dr. Hettler's study on wellness. His mission to help others become aware of the different areas of life helped me look at the quality of my own.

Now at this point, did I immediately stop napping in my car between my college classes? Did I stop pulling all-nighters staying up with my teething toddler while studying for exams? Did I quit one of my two jobs? No, I did not! Nevertheless, I became aware of my behaviors and choices. Awareness, I realized, is the key ingredient to changing anything in one's life. I did connect immediately with Dr. Hettler's mission and began to apply small gestures toward balance to my diaper-book bag of a college life. For instance, instead of downing my usual two-liter bottle of soda in front of open books in the middle of the night, I decided to have two cups of warm green tea. And so my balanced self slowly began to emerge, one small gesture at a time.

Needless to say, I used those original beliefs as my jumping-off point. Those six dimensions of self—spiritual, emotional, physical, social, intellectual, and occupational—guided me on the path to living as I do now and to writing this particular book. Although I may use many of Dr. Hettler's dimensions in a different light with a distinctive twist, they certainly inspired me to think in a more holistic manner. Holistic balance became my passion. I started looking at each of the dimensions thoroughly. I explored each one as though I were taking a full-time course. While obtaining credit hours for my therapy credentials, I began to hold workshops, educating teachers, healing groups, and the incarcerated therapy group I worked with about the dimensions of the self. I became even more awake to my passion once I realized I had started adding my own significant ideas to each of the six aspects. For instance, the occupational dimension became much more than a person's values with his involvement in a career or job. Rather, I began educating others about the importance of how one occupies one's time in this world. I put an emphasis on becoming attentive to your time, on what you put in your mind, what you choose to read and listen to, and how you choose to use your daily hours.

In the following pages, I'll define and discuss each dimension for you in more depth. With each aspect—spiritual, emotional, physical, social, intellectual, and occupational—you will be given an exercise to learn more about yourself. These key dimensions to the whole self will give you a greater understanding of each facet of the deeper you. Balancing each one is a skill, and, when you add your own personal style to it, voilà, you have your whole self, the complete you.

The Whole Self: Who Am I?

Here is an exercise I developed for you to learn more about the real you, the whole self. Please do not hesitate to take a great deal of time on this exercise. It is better to be spontaneous and write down your first thoughts. Take a piece of paper and label it "The Whole Self: Who Am I?" Then number the paper 1 through 6 with these headings:

1. The spiritual dimension
2. The emotional aspect
3. The physical self
4. The social dimension
5. The intellectual aspect
6. The occupational self

Now write one of your roles or an aspect of your life next to each numbered facet. As I mentioned, it is better to write down your first thoughts that come to mind. For example, next to "The spiritual dimension," you might write, "I am a yoga instructor" or "I am a devout Catholic." For "The social dimension," you might state, "I am introverted" or "I am a social butterfly." Regardless, be sure to include something true about yourself as you relate it to each dimension. Continue on through number 6, spontaneously writing down "I am . . ." next to each numbered dimension.

Now that your list is finished, tape it to your chest and walk around for a little while as you reflect on what you put next to each number. Are you happy with your list? Ask yourself, "Who am I really?" Does this list reflect the real you? Would you like to make some changes in it? If so, jot yourself a note next to the area in which you would like to make changes. Draw a star next to what you love about yourself! Keep this list in a folder labeled "The Whole Me." I am certain you will want to return to it as you develop each of your dimensions. It is also healthy for your emotional aspect to look back on your growth and view it as the worthwhile experience it is. There will be many exercises throughout this book to help you uncover your authentic self as you begin to teach others about being their authentic selves. Keep in mind that balance is the key as you continue onward and look at each facet of the whole self.

• • •

The Spiritual Self

The first dimension is defined as the spiritual self. There are many aspects to the spiritual self. Your creativity is based here. It is where all your spontaneity stems from. The connection you feel to your higher power lives in this facet. How you form a relationship with your higher power and how you define your purpose in this universe are relative and extremely personal to each individual.

When you work in a public school system, *creative self* is the politically correct term for the spiritual dimension of a person. You will use the phrase creative self when working with the children. For now, though, I will refer to it as the spiritual self, defined in the broadest sense. Please take note that I am not referring to simply a "religious" self when discussing the spiritual dimension. If you are a religious person, however, that certainly could be included as part of who you are under this aspect. Moreover, I am relating to the spiritual self as the distinctive way you define your true essence, the manner in which you are open and expansive in this world.

I also feel it is essential to illustrate how I remain balanced in this dimension. I am certain that if anyone is stumped in this area, you will be able to find the necessary connections and reminders of what your personal spiritual connection embraces. For me to remain spiritually balanced, I begin with a simple prayer when I open my eyes each day. I say, "Thank you for this morning. Give me strength as I get out of my comfortable bed and all the comforts of my home and go to work out in today's world. Help me to shine in every dimension of my whole self and help others to see their unique beauty and creativity." It usually flows something like this, but you know as well as I do that life is not always the same each morning. On your most tired days you could simply say, "Thank you for this life" or "Thank you for this day." Regardless of my circumstances, I always thank my higher power for each day. Whether you are sad, angry, depressed, exhilarated, or whatever, train your spirit self to never forget that each day truly is precious. It is a gift that you can take a breath today. We never know what the next hour may hold in store for each of us; therefore, this very moment is precious. Still others may feel more comfortable with a simple positive thought, such as, "I'm glad to be alive" or "What gesture can I offer to someone today who needs help?" Regardless of your faith, your practice, or anything in between, begin each day with a simple connection, a spiritual or creative ritual to help you become more aware of this dimension within yourself.

While attending workshops for my therapy credentials, I learned that it takes the mind and the body a minimum of twenty-one to thirty days to form a habit, whether it is a good habit or a bad one. I knew I could apply this research to my spirit as well, and that is what I did. A simple ten-second prayer before you touch your feet to the floor will make an amazing difference in your daily attitude. It truly sets the tone for the day ahead.

There are other ways I remain spiritually balanced. Not only do I talk with my higher power through prayer, but I listen as well. Each day I take several minutes to meditate. I sit in a quiet place, focus on my breath, and take a few moments to become aware of my spirit in my body. I often hear people say they are not quite sure whether they are meditating right. The more you practice meditation and listening to your higher power, the easier it will become for you. There are many great books on all types of meditation (see Additional Resources on page 139). You may find a class at a meditation center or through a community education program. Videos and

DVDs on meditation are also available. Explore meditative tips that you feel connected to. Some people find quiet breathing meditation soothing, while you may feel more connected to walking meditation or a type of nature contemplation. Certainly the Internet is also an amazing resource for finding definitions, types of meditation, local classes, and other connections. Find what works for you. The all-encompassing purpose of any type of meditation discipline is to find quiet time within the moment at hand, to find space with your higher power. I highly recommend any discipline for your spirit's growth.

Yoga is also a path for me to enhance my spiritual development. I practice yoga four to six days a week. I make sure I practice in an open, clean space so that when I am finished, I leave feeling more in touch with who I am spiritually and more open to the world around me. I have taught yoga as well. Teaching yoga has been a way for me to give back what I know about being spiritually balanced. And because it helps others, in return it helps my spirit. By giving we receive. That is the way life works.

• EXERCISE •

The Spiritual Self: Evolving the Healthy Spirit

For your next exercise, begin with a new sheet of paper and title it "The Spiritual Self: Evolving the Healthy Spirit." Below the title, write all the ways you remain spiritually healthy. Under those items, list one or two ways you could improve on your spiritual growth. Keep each idea simple and be specific. Do not simply write, "I will walk outdoors more." Rather, state what is realistic for you. "I will walk outside for fifteen minutes five days a week after dinner." By being specific in your growth plans, you will clearly know your expectations and be able to live up to your own realistic goals. This will help you feel successful as you enhance your spiritual self and grow into the real you.

Remember, all these gestures will add up as you uncover your authentic self. Include this piece in your "Whole Me" folder and occasionally reflect back on it to see the number of small gestures growing.

• • •

The Emotional Self

The emotional self is incredibly involved. It sends messages to all the other dimensions. It lets you know how you are doing spiritually, physically, socially, intellectually, occupationally, and, of course, emotionally. The role of the emotional self is complex, because you may be doing well in your physical and social dimensions but hurting in your intellectual, occupational, and spiritual aspects. Simply put, when you are balanced in all other dimensions, your emotional self is proud, happy, and at peace. Let us first discuss this multifaceted dimension, the emotional self.

It is normal to have all sorts of emotions. It is normal to feel sad, depressed, irritated, overwhelmed, excited, and at peace at various times during the same day. Furthermore, once you understand the nature of emotions, you'll find it is far easier to grasp the complexity of the emotional component of the self. A person I know who is highly involved in Alcoholics Anonymous and other twelve-step programs once told me we can experience more than two hundred feelings. That in itself is amazing. Our feelings convey meaning to all other aspects of our being. Our emotions let us know how we are doing physically. If we are tired, our fatigued and lethargic body will tell us. If we are depressed, our emotional self will look to the spiritual dimension for a way out of the hole. If we are feeling lonely, we will look to our social aspect and ask it for help. If we are lacking in the areas of intellectual and occupational growth, our emotions will tell our bodies about the emptiness we feel deep inside ourselves.

The emotional senses we have work as a funnel, guiding us to a more balanced state of being. It is important to respect and honor the emotional self. Listen to your emotions and, more important, identify them. Listen to the messages your body is sending you.

The Emotional Self: My Feelings Today

Take a moment now to make a list of all the feelings you have had today. Be specific. Rather than writing, "I felt sad," write, "I felt sad when my boss was too busy to tell me what a great job I was doing in my classroom today." By being specific, you can take your power back instead of wallowing in your negative feelings. How do you take your power back? By identifying why you felt a certain way, you can also identify what you can do within your power to change your negativity into a more positive attitude.

In the example I gave, I could have been disheartened all day, sinking in my own sadness. Instead, by pinpointing what was happening, I was able to gather some strength back. By seeing that someone was too busy to notice my contribution, I realized the boss's action did not negate my contribution. Ideally, taking note of the circumstances results in the opposite of being self-pitying. It focuses on the positive. Furthermore, it states that my contribution to the world of teaching was splendid. Nevertheless, I wished someone could have noticed. This acknowledgment alone helps keep depression away. It holds negative feelings at bay and positive feelings at the forefront.

It is important to identify all your feelings and never sweep any of them under the carpet. If you're sad, then by all means be sad. If you're angry, then be angry. I have heard it said that people who get angry are not angry people. This saying expresses so much about the emotional self. By experiencing our feelings, by expressing our emotions, we honor our emotional self. This goes for all feelings, whether you have identified them as negative or positive emotions. Do not hide your negative feelings.

On the other hand, do not hang out in a negative space for long periods of time either. It is more important to identify your feelings and state what needs to be done to move into a more positive frame of mind. In this example, it is better for me to note that I was sad because no one acknowledged my great efforts in the world of teaching today. Then I am able to identify what needs to be done for me to feel better. Sometimes if I feel sad, I need to set a timer and just cry for thirty minutes. Other times I need to find a friend and share what my sad day was about. Taking action will single-handedly relieve most of my sadness, and in effect it will also help balance out the social dimension by honoring friendships as well.

Add this list to your "Whole Me" file. Take special note of any patterns or repeated feelings you had throughout your day. By being aware of your feelings, you have an added advantage to understanding more of your emotional self. This is all done by simply being attentive. Include on this list, next to your identified feelings, any action steps you may wish to take. By merely writing these things down, you are claiming your feelings and identifying the appropriate actions that need to occur for you to get back to balance.

• EXERCISE •

The Emotional Self: Retaining Emotional Health

Make a list of all the ways you remain emotionally healthy. It is important to list all the ways you can freely express yourself. For example, you may include that you are part of a writers' group, keep a personal journal, or have a best friend you consult with about your most private issues. Possibly you dance around your living room and sing loudly when you feel joyous. Or for fun, on your daily drive home, you turn up the volume on your radio so incredibly loud, and sing like there is no tomorrow. Regardless, be sure to truthfully include all the ways you are able to freely express yourself. I am certain that even after you feel your list is complete, you will still identify other ways that you do this. It has simply become a part of you. Afterward, record one or two ways you can improve upon your emotional balance. For example, you may write that the next time you have a gut reaction about a situation, you are not going to discard that feeling. Rather, you will look at the feeling and identify what your body is attempting to reveal to you. Put this list with the others in your "Whole Me" file.

· · ·

The Physical Self

Who are we physically? That may sound like a simple question, yet there is more to the physical dimension than meets the eye. You are more than, for example, the 135-pound female with brown hair and brown eyes or the 180-pound male with light hair and blue eyes that you see in the mirror each day. In addition to this outer body, there are many aspects to the second dimension, the physical self. Let us first examine the obvious part of our physical self, our tangible external body.

Once again, I will reiterate that you must find what works for you to remain "physically" balanced. I will share the ways that work for me, and in doing so I am confident your physical development will become more evident to you.

Overall, I feel balanced physically. I try to get plenty of sleep each night. I exercise four to six days a week to keep my body feeling healthy. I eat a balanced diet full of fruits and vegetables, grains, nuts, and cheese, and all the good stuff you already know about. Certainly, I balance it out with my favorite occasional treats of key lime pie, chocolate peanut butter bars, and buttered popcorn too. For the most part, though, I come from a balanced state of physical health. Yes, the periodic indulgences will happen; however, they will be more on a conscious level and done in a balanced manner. Awareness is a key factor to balance within all of the dimensions.

Another way I remain physically healthy is by striving not to be extremely critical about my physical body. Instead, I do the best I can at taking care of my physical appearance. I get plenty of rest, I drink lots of water, and I pamper myself with hot baths. Nourish your physical body. Even as I am getting ready for work in the morning, I do nurturing things for my physical self, like a bit of meditation and exercise. Try always to remember that your body is thankful for the smallest gesture you can offer it. After a calming hot bath, I apply makeup modestly and try to highlight my better features. Do not look in the mirror and notice all the flaws the physical body naturally comes with. Preferably put the focus on your strong points—and, by the way, each physical body does come with strong points.

For example, when you look in the mirror, try to be aware of your thoughts. If they are negative, which thoughts can be at times, and you begin to think "My nose is too big" or something of that nature, quickly change your message to "I like my cheekbones" or something more positive. Focusing on the positive is a key within all the dimensions of the self and of life. Focus on the positive. This will help you in your response to your physical dimension.

Besides an outer physical self, we also have an inner physical self, which holds a great deal of wisdom. Our inner wisdom is very involved and complex. My yoga experience has furthered my knowledge of this fact. I cannot tell you enough how important it is to listen to your body. If your body is tired, it will tell you. If it is hungry, it will tell you. If it is not hungry, it will say so as well. Your body radiates all kinds of feelings to you all the time. Your feelings and thoughts create body messages and energy in a variety of ways. It is important that you listen to those messages and honor them. Your mind has been trained for years and years by a chaotic society with irrational people in it. It is more important now that you listen to your body's wisdom.

Let me give you an example of this principle. I grew up in a blue-collar home. My dad worked the eleven to seven shift as a dock loader, and my mom worked swing shifts taking care of elderly patients in a hospital and in private care. When I was young, I recall my dad saying he had not missed work in eleven years. I also remember my mom going to work very ill. She would say, "I am sicker than a dog and I am going to work. There's no reason anyone needs to get out of going to work." In other words, she was in essence saying, do not listen to the messages of your body, but comply with the craziness of society's demands and go to work. It deserves mention that my dad died at forty-two and my mom at fifty-two. Their messages still lie ingrained in my mind. When my body knows not to go to work it tells me, "Your throat is scratchy, your body is tense from all the stress, and furthermore, you are exhausted from the unbelievable demands that are put on teachers these days." My body screams, "You need to take this time and return yourself to health!" Nevertheless, to this day I still have to argue with my mind to take a day off and nurture myself back to health. Why? Mostly because many people still come from that irrational state of mind, as my mom and dad once did, trying to keep moving whether they are sick or not.

• EXERCISE •

The Physical Self: Awareness of the Physical Body

How do I maintain my body physically when we live in a society where the minority is thin and the majority is overweight? How do I preserve myself when we are confronted with an abundance of temptation each day on television, in the advertisements we read, in the grocery stores, and everywhere around us? Try these two approaches I use to touch base with myself physically to stay aware.

Ask yourself if you "see" yourself. Use the acronym SEE—Sleep, Exercise, Eat—to check in with yourself regarding your overall physical balance. Ask yourself, "Am I getting a healthy amount of sleep? Am I getting the proper amount of exercise for my physical body? And am I eating a healthy array of foods in a balanced way?" Keep a daily SEE journal and include it in your "Whole Me" file. Record these basic items in your notebook: the quantity and quality of sleep you get each day; the amount and type of daily exercise you had; what you had to eat and drink daily, including all snacks and meals. Keep it very simple for quick referencing. It should be the first document you look at when you feel out of sorts. If your physical body is undernourished, you will have it on record and actually note the action steps you need to take to get back to balance. Include the action steps in your SEE journal when necessary.

Another thing I try to do on a daily basis is to be aware of my eating and drinking habits. I do this in several ways. Try this technique for enhancing your conscious physical health. Make an effort each time you put anything into your body to ask, "Does this help my body to be balanced and have positive energy?" In your SEE journal, include a list of items that give you great positive energy. Separately list items that do not agree with you and overall negatively affect you. Take note of what to avoid and what to include more of in your life for balanced energy. In addition to raising your awareness, this will also help you to be more thankful for what you do have.

• EXERCISE •

The Physical Self: Staying Healthy

Make a list of all the ways you remain physically healthy. Below those items, write down three ways you can improve your physical health. Include all this in your "Whole Me" folder. Once again, be specific. Instead of writing, for example, "I will get more sleep, I will cut back on sweets, and I will also exercise more," it is better to write, "I will go to bed each night by nine thirty and I will only allow dessert three times a week. I will also exercise five times a week for thirty minutes." By being specific, you will be able to see the results happen. By feeling the success, you are already successful.

Certainly it is important not to expect the immediate results and instant gratification that the unbalanced world holds so very dear. Rather, it is more valuable for you to commit to healthy balance. Continue to make these daily gestures toward it. To recap, it takes the mind at least twenty-one to thirty days to form a habit. Remind yourself often of this information as you train yourself to be the physically balanced human being you need to be.

• • •

The Social Self

Who are you socially? Are you the cynic at work and home? Are you the quiet one? Are you a bubbly person others enjoy being around? Regardless of which one you think you are now, it is more important to identify the type of person you want to be and why you want to be that person socially. Being the authentic person you are meant to be is more important than any popularity contest you may be playing in your mind. To put it simply, there will be days when you may be off balance and a little on the cynical side or simply more reserved than usual; nevertheless, you will do the work necessary to get yourself back in a positive, balanced framework.

Personally, I am more extroverted than my husband. He would just as soon stay home for the most part, unless it is to attend a hockey game. Because of our differences, we have had to balance our social calendars. I, as well as he, know the importance of fellowship and feeling connected to others. We set aside time each month to get together with friends for dinner and to simply socialize. We almost always comment on what a good time we had. Human beings are social beings, and it is important to honor that element of our existence.

The social self has many facades. Today, we play many roles and juggle too many priorities. We have almost forgotten why we are here and what our purpose is. I believe our true purpose is to combine our unique self with other authentic individuals to make a healthy world for everyone involved. Instead, we put on our work role in the morning, our parenting role in the evening, and our neighborly role over the weekend. By that time we are exhausted and, more important, have discounted the fact that there is a spirit in us that wants to be genuine.

The Social Self: My Effective Social Characteristics

Make a list of all the roles you play on a daily basis, for example, parent, teacher, spouse, and sister. Next to each role identify all the characteristics that go along with that role. The characteristics next to parent may be strict, loving, helpful, angry, and self-righteous. The characteristics next to sister may be something like superior, patronizing, loving, and helpful. Now circle all the ineffective characteristics for which you would not like to be identified. You may have circled the angry and self-righteous characteristics under the parent role and also the superior and patronizing characteristics under the sister role. By simply being aware of which characteristics you would like to diminish, you heighten your social awareness. By and large, this is a major step to helping and healing your social dimension.

Now consider how you remain socially balanced. How often do you attend social functions? And, more important, how often do you attend social functions as the real you? Do you go out socially? If yes, how often? These are questions to ponder as you reflect on the individual characteristics for which you wish to be identified. Knowing who you are and what traits you would like to be known for is critical to developing your social persona. Include this paper with your social information in your "Whole Me" folder.

● ● ●

The Intellectual Self

An intellectual person is basically someone who spends time thinking and studying about the world around her. I am a very intellectual person. I did not realize that until I was in my later twenties, after I had completed my undergraduate work and found a job as a schoolteacher. It was then that I felt my intellectual success.

Beforehand and in my early teen years, I actually felt somewhat naive. My world during my school years was predominantly a social one. My whole self was way off balance. The social dimension was seemingly my only interest, and I did not give much attention to the other aspects of the self. My world was friends, dances (I never missed one), sporting events, boyfriends, and whatever social event was happening the coming weekend. I disconnected from the academic intellectual aspect, and I got by. Looking back I understand how school personnel found it easier to allow me to go down this narrow pathway than to reinvigorate me with encouraging academic knowledge and the outlook of a successful future.

It was not until my first year of college that I realized I had always had an innate intellectual desire. My first English professor read some of my work and told me of my gift of persuasive writing. He encouraged me to write and excitedly asked when he could read more of my work. A science professor suggested that I should be a scientist because of my natural curiosity. These types of messages turned my world around. I became an intellectual sponge, partly because of the newfound messages that surrounded me. I instilled these new statements in myself, thus growing in more ways than one. Needless to say, I ended up graduating cum laude with a high grade point average. If you were to ask any of my high school teachers five years prior whether that was possible, I am not sure any of them would have bet on it. Nonetheless, proactive remarks are more important than ever in today's world, and they are what we need to give our children.

It is no wonder today's teenagers have such severe issues. Discipline, positive guidance, and awareness have slipped into the background while instant gratification and immersing themselves in what they want, when they want it, seem to be the norm for today's young population. As a society, we have allowed our children to go down any path of their choosing, because it is just easier to let them to do so, even if it is to their detriment. Eating disorders, depression, and suicide attempts, basically all their cries for help, along with their drug and alcohol addictions, are pervasive in schools today. The same old wounding, negative messages that lack direction and attention are overflowing in today's unbalanced world. In fact, they are now spilling over more rapidly because of the crazy, busy world in which we are living. Adults seem more hectic, reacting to this type of world. Nevertheless providing guidance and full attention to our young people is most critical now.

Today's youth are our greatest resource in turning this unbalanced world around. It is possible to recover from this damage and heal the world. We need to do this by reviving their innate intellectualism in their hearts. I once took a reading course that taught that if you want children to read, teach them to believe they can read. To connect this premise to the intellectual dimension, I believe we need to teach children about their inherent wisdom. We need to teach them to believe in their intellectual selves. We need to show them how their bodies hold wisdom, how their minds are sharp and can identify the good judgments they need to make. We need to show them their spirits can soar. This is the job of today's teacher. It is critical that we fulfill this obligation.

• EXERCISE •

The Intellectual Self: Wisely Balanced

How do you remain intellectually balanced? On a separate piece of paper for the intellectual dimension, write down the things you do in your life to improve your intellectual self. How do you broaden yourself as an intellectual being? Include one or two action steps you can take to strengthen the intellectual dimension in your life. Add this to the other papers in your "Whole Me" file.

• • •

The Occupational Self

In my deeper understanding, the occupational self is much more than a job and employment. It is about how we occupy our time in this world. I hadn't realized this until the first time I held a workshop on the dimensions of the self in which a retired person was in attendance. I could tell by her reaction that she was still mourning her lack of employment as she worked her way into retirement. When I presented an exercise about how people remained occupationally balanced in their lives, she told me her occupational self was "dead." When I changed the wording to how do you "occupy" your time in your life, I could tell she felt much better. This was also my turning point when looking at the occupational aspect of the self.

I look at the occupational self as a link to the spiritual component. I occupy my time in many ways, and those activities usually connect with the spiritual dimension. Of course, in my actual job, I occupy my time as a teacher, and, more important, I do this on a more meaningful level. First, I am a teacher of how to be a balanced human being. Next, I am an elementary school teacher. I occupy my time with writing. I spend time decorating for the holidays with my family. I also occupy my time with leisurely Sundays. I take yoga and teach it to others twice a week. I spend time scrapbooking and reflecting on memories with family and friends. I do jobs that keep my household flowing smoothly, such as laundry, cooking, paying bills, and grocery shopping. I occupy some of my time daydreaming in a hammock. I also work in the garden. These are some of the ways I use my time in the occupational dimension of myself.

I think it is important to explain what I aim *not* to do with my occupational component. I make an effort not to occupy my time with meaningless things, such as worrying and complaining. Furthermore, I strive to be in the moment and focus on the tasks at hand.

The Occupational Self: Making Wishful Behaviors Happen

For your next exercise, fold a piece of paper in half lengthwise. On one side, make a list of all the ways you occupy your time. Of course, include your employment and all your avocations. Name all the behaviors that occupy your time as well. Now on the other side of the paper, list other ways you wish to occupy your time. Next to each wishful way, write one step you can take to make that occupation come alive in your life.

Remember to be specific. This will help you be successful within the occupational dimension. Include this new information in your "Whole Me" folder. You should now have exercises for the whole you and for each dimension of the whole self. It will be a fabulous resource to reflect back on as you continue to watch your growth happen.

• • •

By being a mindful person, you are adding awareness, which is greatly needed in today's unbalanced world. The aware teacher thinks logically and creates with wisdom. Today's children are yearning for these types of adults. Aware people coming from this healthy space are the first ingredient for a balanced tomorrow.

2

Exude Positive Energy

If the world seems cold to you, kindle fires to warm it!
—Lucy Larcom, 1824–93, American suffragist, feminist

The teacher is the one to establish the atmosphere in the classroom. Enthusiasm and a positive attitude are contagious energies that inspire virtually everyone. I find it's important to point out that insensitivity and a negative attitude are infectious as well. The teacher sets the tone. How you choose to spend your days in the classroom is up to you. If you decide to have a positive attitude, you continually strengthen and balance all the dimensions of the whole self. Think about it. Spiritually, it is uplifting to look at the glass as half full. Emotionally, your feelings become optimistic and hopeful. Physically, your focus is on your positive attributes. Socially, you enjoy friends and family with a pleasant manner. Intellectually, the world you study becomes a place full of possibilities. And with a positive attitude, your occupational self is at peace with the activities you engage in. A positive person is a joy to be around.

How do you change your attitude to be more positive? How do you speak positively in a faculty room when seemingly the only forms of talk are negative conversations? The talk is usually about the school, the administrators, the work, and, of course, all the difficult children. The demands, the gossip, and the complaints drain the teachers' energy, leaving them depleted and feeling negative about their livelihood. The teachers leave the faculty room after lunch and wonder how much longer they can go on like this. When in fact, if the talk had been more positive, upbeat, and inspirational, they would leave feeling revived and light. That spirit would then journey back to the classroom to continue encouraging others.

As an undergraduate, I often heard my professors give advice on not becoming involved in shoptalk in the school's faculty rooms. I have since heard from inspirational education speakers, colleagues, and others that often these places can be full of people who are part of the BMW club. The BMW club is not made up of teachers driving fancy cars. It actually stands for the Bitch, Moan, and Whine group. In my early years of teaching, I learned exactly what they were talking about. But what do we do about the tendency to complain?

First, understanding the nature of negative thoughts and behavior is important. This brings awareness, and awareness is the key to finding your positive outlook. People who are negative and complain for the most part are in a sense searching for happiness. They are generally pessimistic, and when they connect with other unhappy individuals, it creates an illusion of pleasure. The illusion is this: if I complain with you, then we are all in this together; therefore, my life is full of friends. In actuality, the true picture is closer to hell. In some weird sense, this commiserating behavior makes the social self feel somewhat satisfied, even though it leaves all the other dimensions depleted and hungry for balance. A true friend would help you get out of the hole and into a positive frame of mind. A true friend on occasion may have a bad day herself and need to vent, but for the most part shares in creating goodness. Overall, connectedness should be reviving and vitalizing to the self. Be attentive to the words you use. Positive thoughts and positive talk evoke positive energy. Furthermore, they help even the most challenging of situations.

A Positive Approach

It is important not only for you as the teacher to have a positive attitude but also for you to focus on the positive attributes of the children. Research shows that students respond better when the teacher focuses on a student's positive trait rather than complaining about a negative behavior. For example, if a child is misbehaving by talking nonstop when you are trying to teach a lesson, it is better to reward another child for respectful listening skills. Obviously the disrespectful child is seeking attention. When he realizes you noticed another child's good behavior, chances are the misbehaving child will begin to listen in hopes of being recognized too. When that happens, it is important that you immediately acknowledge the challenging student's good behavior. This helps change the negative into more positive behavior.

In my first month of teaching, I conformed to what other colleagues were doing regarding discipline. I wanted to fit in as a first-year teacher, so I abided by a discipline plan that had been in place for years. The discipline plan in kindergarten had to do with a stop sign and check marks. Whenever children were "naughty," their names were put in a stop sign. If the children continued with their misbehavior, check marks were put next to their names. If they received a certain number of check marks, privileges were taken away. When a special activity called "Fabulous Friday" came at the end of the week, the "naughty" children were sent to a nap room. Teachers were allowed to send up to five students from their classroom to the nap area. Not all teachers complied with this rule, however; they would send as many as seven, eight, or nine children. Needless to say, the nap room was always full. This sort of discipline plan is reactive. In other words, the students would misbehave and then the teachers would react to that negative misbehavior. It was a strategy I strongly disagreed with. After a month of implementing it, I had to forgo the system because it simply did not mesh with my personal philosophy of education.

Granted, there are times when a teacher does need to deal with a severe behavior problem, and she must react to an act of violence or something of that nature. Nine times out of ten, though, the misbehaving occurs for one of three reasons, as I learned from Lee Canter, the creator of various education courses and books on succeeding with difficult children. According to Canter, the first reason for misbehavior is that the child is seeking attention—and giving children positive attention is the best practice for teachers and students in handling this. The second reason is that the tasks you are asking the child to do are either too difficult or too easy, which means the child lacks motivation and the teacher may have to modify the task at hand. The third reason is that the student needs boundaries and straightforward positive practices in place, so the teacher may need to provide firm limits and simple rules to live by, including reminding children to respect themselves, respect others, and respect all things.

To reiterate, first the child is seeking attention. Second, the child lacks motivation, because the work is too hard or actually not challenging enough. Or third, the student needs firm limits. All of these reasons should be taken care of in a proactive manner. Students respond better when a teacher uses a proactive approach. Furthermore, it works for any age level. How do you apply this approach? Included next are my ideas for keeping the focus on the positive, which is a constructive and beneficial approach to discipline and classroom management.

The Good Behavior Picture

Children like to hear their names, and when you add a positive comment with their name, voilà, a little positive classroom management occurs. This is how you use "The Good Behavior Picture" idea with children in prekindergarten and early primary grades. At the beginning of the year, take a camera around during cleanup time. As you see children cleaning up, announce it as you take a Good Behavior Picture. Say, for example, "I like the way Brandon is cleaning up the blocks." He will look up and smile for your camera. As children clean up, or not, you go around the classroom announcing, "I am looking to see if I can take some more Good Behavior Pictures." I am certain the children will scramble around to clean up so that they can have their pictures taken too. This especially helps with your most challenging students who were not focused on this task at first.

Continue taking pictures throughout the first month of school until you have captured in photos all the children making good choices at cleanup time. After you develop the pictures or print them out from your computer, put them together in a classroom book and add captions, such as "Miguel picked up the puzzles." Be sure to include all the children in this classroom book. Refer to your book throughout the year to promote responsible behavior within the classroom. As you can see, your book can be used for early primary reading purposes too. Therefore, it provides a way to instruct early emergent reading skills as well as positive character education traits.

Throughout the year, you can use a modification of the Good Behavior Picture idea. You can do it with your students' imaginations, this time without a camera. For instance, during a transition time, let's say it is cleanup time, you would hold up your hands as though you are truly holding a camera and peeking through your hands' opening at a positive behavior. You would say, "I like the way Maria is picking up the scraps and putting her supplies away. Smile, Maria! Click!" Just watch as the other children start to pick up their supplies and throw scraps away. They too want to hear their names called out in a positive way. Challenging students who are seeking attention would rather hear their names in a positive way than in a negative one. The Good Behavior Picture honors the positive behavior and gets children who are misbehaving back on task.

Please remember to immediately recognize any of the challenging students who get back on task. This helps teach children to use more positive behavior independently and more often.

The Shape, Number, and Other Sorts of Clubs

Instead of using a stop sign or another type of warning sign as a discipline technique, try using a membership club. This classroom management technique has proved to work for me time and time again.

Because younger children need to learn about shapes, you might try a shape club. Simply draw a shape on the chalkboard and label it "The Circle Club" or whatever shape you are working on. I even taught the days of the week by labeling a drawing "The Monday Circle Club" and changing the card daily to correspond to each day of the week. Next to the shape club, include students' names on pieces of construction paper that have been cut into that shape. Put a magnet on the back of each shape so each student's name can be moved into the shape club when a student is "caught being good." For example, if you see Trevor picking up toys, simply say out loud for the entire class to hear, "Trevor, go put your name in our Monday Circle Club, because you are picking up the toys and making good choices." The children who were not picking up and following the rules will now begin to pick up. If you see one of your challenging students beginning to follow the rules, ask him to also put his name in the shape club.

Soon all the children will want to have their names in the Circle Club. Why? The children who make it in will get a simple reward sometime during the course of the day. I have treated children with a special place to read during reading time, a special teddy bear to sleep with during naptime, and anything else that is simple yet rewarding for the children. This technique of focusing on the positive is a constructive way of encouraging students who are not making good choices to immediately choose a better option. And when those same students receive a little recognition for their better options, they fill their need for attention in a positive manner.

Emily is putting her name in the Oval Club. She knows she will get a special treat for making good choices at school.

As the children grow older, you can use the same format as the shape club but modify it to meet older students' interests. In a different grade level, I use a number club. In older grades, you can use a word club or whatever else you are working on, such as an adjective club. Call it the "Brilliant Club" one week and the "Astounding Club" the next. On a small area of the chalkboard, simply write the word *brilliant* and include a box underneath it. As you notice "brilliant" behavior that week, write the students' names in the box. Instilling positive messages in children's minds is another way to help balance our world. Besides, it keeps classroom management on a positive note. Keep changing adjectives week after week. You will be providing children with today's necessary positive reinforcement and a repertoire of new vocabulary words too.

I have even created Zipper and Tying Clubs to give younger children the incentive to learn these fine-motor skills early in life. I recall years ago while I was student teaching that my early primary sponsor teacher, Christine Huggler-Wyant, would encourage children who were working on zipping their own coats, by saying, "Let's try and make it in my Zipper Club!" Years later, I came up with the idea to put a real zippered vest on an oversized cardboard hanger, label it "Mrs. Fishbaugh's Zipper Club," and hang it in the classroom. As children independently zipped their own coats at dismissal time, I would add their names on labels to the vest. The Zipper Club encouraged independence and gave others the incentive to attempt their own zipping and independence. Such a process not only helps children know a simple basic life skill but also raises their self-esteem and empowers them. All these small gestures add great balance to our world.

Treasure Chest

During my first year of teaching, I began to keep a shoebox of goodies next to my rocking chair. Later, I labeled it "Miss Schmidt's Goodies." It was primarily for children who were "caught being good," although I also used it with unruly children to immediately change their behavior and give them a second chance. During group time or transition time, I would allow some children who were making good choices, and students who immediately changed their negative behavior into positive behavior, to pick a treat out of the box. Items such as Tootsie Rolls, bouncy balls, lollipops, pencils, and miscellaneous toys my son no longer wanted went into this box. It became such a marvelous discipline technique for recognizing positive behavior that occasion-

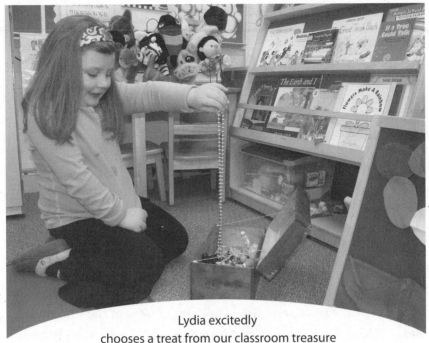

Lydia excitedly chooses a treat from our classroom treasure chest. Today, Lydia gets a treat because she was showing her respectful dining manners at breakfast time. She will be able to take her prize home and share how she made respectful choices in the classroom to earn her treasure chest treat.

ally you would see me walk down the hall with it when I was taking the children to art, gym, or another special event. The students would be unbelievably quiet in hopes of receiving a treat from my goody box. I used my box so much it became warped and fell apart. I decided to have a wooden box made and engraved. Years later, it is now labeled "Mrs. Fishbaugh's Treasure Chest Treats," because it looks like a treasure chest. Furthermore, the one- or two-cent treats really are treasures for the children.

It is important to remember that treasure chest treats are to be used when you see positive behavior happening. It is also important to apply this positive reinforcement technique immediately when you see negative behavior transform into positive conduct.

My Favorite Magical "Handy" Ideas

Not only are young children kinetic learners, they are tactile learners as well. "Handy" ideas are techniques used with the hands to keep children active, involved, and positive. I have several reinforcement ideas that involve the hands. These ideas are inexpensive to use, yet worthy because of their results.

The Magic Handshake

The first handy idea came to me when I ran out of treasure chest treats and a child who made it into my shape club asked me what his treat was for being good today. I recall feeling kind of disappointed. I had in a weird sense trained my students to always expect a tangible item for being good. I was worried that I had not instilled the intrinsic value of simply making good choices. Thinking fast, I told the child to come to the carpet and I would tell him in front of the whole class what his treat was. As the children sat crossed-legged, they quietly and patiently waited to see what the treat would be. I know they thought it might be a pocket toy or something of that nature. Instead, I had the little boy stand by my rocking chair, and I explained I did not have any treasure chest treats left. I saw the disappointment come over his face. I immediately told him that I had something better. Disappointment disappeared. I told him the treat was called a magic handshake. The children looked around at each other. They had never heard of such a treat. I wondered what they thought. Acting surprised and shocked that no one had ever heard of a magic handshake, I informed them that this was their lucky day, because I was going to show them a magic handshake. I told the child to close his eyes and remember back to how good he felt when he made it into the shape club. A faint smile appeared on his face. I told him we had to spin him around three times. He smiled some more. The children on the carpet were smiling now too. When he stopped, I told him to open his eyes and hold out his right hand. He did. Then I told him to place it on his heart and repeat after me. "In my heart, I know I did a great job today at making good choices. This is one of the highest rewards I can have. When I shake Mrs. Fishbaugh's hand, a sensational feeling will come over me because I made good choices." I asked him if he was ready for that incredible feeling to come over him. He nodded his head. I again asked him if he was sure. He nodded his head and held out his hand. As I shook his hand, I smiled and asked if he could feel goodness come over him. He, of course, said yes, because young children always feel magic. Meanwhile, I told the children I would be looking for other children who might deserve a magic handshake today.

Needless to say, children enjoy being magical. And this technique is also a way of helping instill intrinsic values in our young population. Often the children are searching for that extrinsic item, such as a toy or a sticker, for making good choices. The magic handshake focuses on the "good feeling" when they make positive choices. It helps children develop a sense of intrinsic worth.

Magic Dream Lotion

I use other handy ideas that seem quite magical. For instance, I bought a special lotion dispenser that had an enchanted look about it and filled it with scented antibacterial lotion. When I caught someone making great choices in the classroom, I would give that child a small amount of "magic" hand lotion that helps dreams come true. And just between us adults, it not only helps with classroom management but it also keeps germs at bay.

To work the magic, I will simply announce so the whole class can hear that Ellen is receiving magic lotion because she is making good choices today. I ask her to close her eyes and think of a special dream. I then put a small amount on her hand and tell her to rub and rub while she thinks of her dream. When she's finished, I tell her to hold her hands up to her nose and once again breathe in the magic. The children love this aromatic technique. Soon all the children begin to make better choices in hopes of getting some magic lotion as well.

Magic Mist

Another handy idea is for use during the hot, end-of-the-school-year months. When the heat and humidity come into the classroom, I have "magic" mist spray in a special decanter bottle. If children are making good choices, I mist their hands and wrists with cool water from this bottle, which stays in the refrigerator at night and on my desk during the day. As I spray the mist, I inform them it will help them think positive, good thoughts. Once again, the other children want a little of that mist as well. Therefore, any negative behavior transforms into more positive behavior. Furthermore, it gets children thinking optimistic thoughts. Sometimes it is best to put the bottle back in the refrigerator to keep the water cool. You can announce as you are walking to get it, "I'm going to get my magic mist from the refrigerator. I hope I can find some children making good choices. I sure would like to give out some magic today!"

•   •   •

All of these ideas are about finding the positive. I have found that when I take this type of proactive approach, the spiritual and emotional dimensions of my self remain balanced. Furthermore, I have come to realize that I do not come home from work physically drained when I use these types of techniques. If I had merely reacted to negative behavior throughout my day, my physical self would be exhausted and depleted. Intellectually and in my heart, I know that focusing on the positive is obviously much better for my colleagues, the students, and me as well. I occupy my time using proactive measures instead of reactive ways that drain our energy. These techniques focus on the positive, helping the teacher's and students' whole selves remain balanced.

3

Create a Classroom Haven

*The best and most beautiful things in the world cannot be
seen nor even touched, but just felt in the heart.*
—Helen Keller, 1880–1968, American author, lecturer

Through my years of teaching, each fall I have held an open house
to meet my new students and their families. I have held curriculum
information nights and of course have done many parent-teacher
conferences. One particular curriculum night comes to mind, because
I changed the visual atmosphere of my room from that day forth.

I recall being a little nervous the evening before this event, even
though I had done these informative nights in past years. A colleague
with many teaching years asked me how I was doing an hour or two
before the children and their families arrived. I told her the truth:
"I'm nervous." I told her I wanted to make a good impression, so I was
reviewing the report card assessments to share with parents. What
she said next astounded me. She told me not to be nervous because
most of the parents were "losers." She said most of them "do not know
anything you are saying" and overall are "idiots." She also said I could
basically make up my whole evening and tell them anything I wanted

and they "would not know the difference." I stood there momentarily with my mouth open, not quite knowing how to respond. To confess, I am always trying to improve upon this area of my social aspect, to have faster comebacks and quick-wittedness. On that day, I simply replied, "I will try not to remember any of that!" Needless to say, I am generally happy with how I strive to remain positive even with the most severely negative people. Off the experienced teacher went, chuckling, trying to understand whether I was joking with her. I still felt quite dumbfounded and hoped I would never turn that disgracefully cynical and miserable in the teaching profession. The woman who made such outlandish and degrading comments had been a teacher for more than thirty years at that time.

To cut this woman a minuscule slice of slack, because I know the world is hungry for slackcutting, too, I must say that she was probably responding to the parents who are borderline abusive to their children. Even so, I was not interested in her talk, although on a higher level of thinking, I deeply knew her response was to the neglectful and addictive adults who are not good parents. Instead of passing judgments and stereotyping parents, she could have just explained more specifically what she meant. But I must call a spade a spade. After all, I am a parent and I show up for the meet-your-teacher nights at my children's school. And I am smart and not a "loser," as the cynical teacher put it; therefore, I thought, "She must be wrong!" I believe she was trying to connect with me. Unfortunately, her ways of connecting had to do with negative energy filled with griping and judgments.

It was a small turning point for me. During those first years of teaching and encountering pessimistic people, I realized there is always hope, even for the most abusive and addictive person. I know intellectually that sometimes a person has to fall very low before getting up and seeing the light. The teacher who made unkind remarks regarding less fortunate and unbalanced individuals actually taught me something. She taught me what not to be like and what not to do.

Afterward, I began to hang posters in my room to remind myself of the person I aspired to be. I wanted to be a person full of hope, even within the most despairing situations. I wanted people to know me as the positive-energy woman who loves this life. My room became like a big bumper sticker. "This is who I am!" it screamed.

I also noticed that because I am a teacher on this deeper level, I wanted to share and help teach others how to be balanced by posting signs for them as well. And, of course, I wanted to help our youngsters develop their sense of self and feelings. So I created signs for them too. I also formed a "thinking area," which I'll describe to you shortly.

While in college, I had learned the importance of having a language-rich room. The basic philosophy is to hang all sorts of language-rich items in the classroom so children are immersed in the power of the written word. This, of course, helps children read and write in their world. I decided to add to this language-rich theme. I was determined to create a language-rich room that would also be a visual inspirational haven. I wanted my room to reflect my balance, and I wanted it to echo a warm, peaceful learning environment. I wanted it to be a visual place full of cues and messages that would always help even the most distressed person. I know I have succeeded in doing this, because most people who enter my room have similar comments: "Your room is so cheerful" or "This room always feels inviting." Since those early years of my teaching, I have developed my room and ideas even more. Here are some of the visual ideas I use to keep myself and the students motivated, inspired, and encouraged as we live in this unbalanced world.

Visual Cues

I have inspirational posters and sticky notes and little positive messages virtually everywhere in my classroom. A miniature inspirational calendar sits on my desk and offers me wise words for today's teacher.

A poster hanging on my supply cupboard states, "Follow your heart and your dreams will come true." Motivating miniposters that I have typed and printed out from my computer are taped in my classroom where I can view them easily. My favorite poster is on my filing cabinet, given to me by a friend who always tells me, "The children of this world need you." Her poster to me shows an old-fashioned milk jug and reads, "Cream rises to the top." Over the years, especially on my most frenzied days, I have put my weary elbows on my desk and rested my head in my palms and looked deep into that poster. That's when I would begin to fantasize about writing an educational book to help teachers, parents, and children. I would dream of how I would provide workshops to inspire others. Interestingly enough, here I am. I ended up here. That is what I actually did. I followed my heart and read my daily visual cues and lingered on this inspired, balanced path where I want to be.

My home is like this as well. Inspirational messages are here and there whispering my purpose back to me. Even in my downstairs bathroom I have a prayer that you can view while doing your business. It describes letting go of negativity. While you wash your hands, there is also a beautifully framed postcard, which I got from the top-floor gift shop at the World Trade Center in 1993. So its significance means more to me in this century than anyone will ever know. This picture shows two naked little boys from the side, one black and the other white. One is peeing in the sand, and the other is looking down and observing it. This art piece represents the connection we should all feel to one another. If you disagree, well, chalk it up to my art certification coming out. Regardless, we all feel, we all are human, we are all doing these daily things on this earth. Putting up visual cues to help remind you of this is a great thing to do. Everyone who has ever used my downstairs bathroom always comes out and says something along the lines of "I like your bathroom."

I have created a tasteful way of providing just the right number of cues to keep me positive, light, and full of joy. These posters, messages, and special treats are visual prompts to get me back on balance and to love the life I am in at this very moment. Some common themes I have found can remind virtually anyone how to remain positively balanced. Included next are other personal ways I send positive messages to my spirit as well.

Let me begin with my desk and work area, where I do most of my busy paperwork and the not-so-fun aspects of teaching, such as report cards, critical indicators, and benchmarks. In the center of my desk I have a laminated prayer that touches me deeply and reminds me of my purpose. It is the first thing I see when I sit down at my desk. Also included on my desk are pictures of my family. They are peaceful images to look at it when I am feeling stressed from the daily pressures of teaching. I also have a large ceramic mug I drink water from throughout the day. It is a beautiful artsy piece I got from the college where I graduated. It sits on a distinctive coaster. My mug serves two purposes: it helps me enjoy the water I need to drink daily, and it reminds me of my educational accomplishments. I also have some special scented lotion I keep on my desk. This can spontaneously become the magic lotion you may want for your children when a quick sense of classroom management is needed. Throughout the day, I occasionally put some on, and as I do, I remind myself to treasure the simple pleasures of this life.

I have a sticky note that states, "I determine my priorities." This of course reminds me that I am in control of my calendar and do not need to say yes to every request and event that come my way. Instead, I choose activities that help me feel most balanced and spirit-filled. Once again, it is a way of being well adjusted and taking charge of my own life.

Other visual cues help me have an attitude of gratitude. On my computer I have a little trinket of a man balancing on a rope. This reminds me to dedicate time to my writing passion. Taped to my computer is a flyer that simply reminds, "Have a Positive Attitude." Also in the computer area is another flyer stating, "Positive People Do Not Put

Others Down." I specifically made this one for a woman who comes into my room passing judgments on others. All of these are little re- minders to stay aware and be positive.

Once a friend of mine sent me a birthday card on which she wrote that I was a "shining star." Included in the envelope was a half-inch gold star. I glued it to the top center frame of my doorway. I doubt anyone else has ever noticed it, but it reminds me of my purpose to shine. I have so many other posters, quotations, and notes too numer- ous to mention, but here are a few more of the visual inspirational reminders that help me love this life:

- Be Kind.
- Treat Others the Way You Want to Be Treated.
- Dare to Take Risks.
- Need Less.
- If I am to die, then how shall I live?
- Celebrate!
- "Nothing can bring you peace but yourself."
  —Ralph Waldo Emerson
- Slow Down.
- Be Good to Yourself.
- LIVE LIFE.
- "Dwell as near as possible to the channel in which
  your life flows."—Henry David Thoreau
- Be a human being, not a human doing.

And a favorite, which continues to inspire me:

- Never be afraid to shine who you are!

All of these little heartfelt visual reminders have helped me con- tinue on my path, keep a balanced perspective, and love the life that is in front of me. They work for me. Try creating a few inspirational prompts that work for you and keep you positive, balanced, and lov- ing this life. Begin by adding a few visual cues to some special area or sacred space in your home. This will help as you start your day and head off to the work world. Then add cues to your work area too. Include these visual inspirational items around the space where you do your busy work. Changing them from time to time also provides a bit of freshness.

Character Education Activities

I always like to begin my school year with a lesson in how to work peacefully and cooperatively with one another. It not only sets the tone for the year, it also is a basic life skill that many individuals never truly learn. I enjoyed one character education activity in particular, because it helped make my room peaceful and warm the whole year through. It sent a visual reminder of peace to me, my students, and to anyone else who saw it.

I remember the actual day I felt inspired to do this activity. While visiting another school, I saw the word *peace* in banner size on a classroom wall. The word alone felt inspiring and so did the pictures that went along with it. "We need more of this in our unbalanced world," I thought. I immediately filed it away in the large folder in my head labeled "Creative teaching ideas to implement someday." A few years later, I came across this mindful idea again. It was hidden under the stack of overcluttered theme-related folders labeled "Help me . . . I'm an early primary teacher" and "What was I thinking when I chose my major?" I tossed these confused, muddled folders into the garbage, brought the positive folder to the front, and began to thumb through it. I was happy to find it again. It was the glimmer of hope I needed.

That day I asked my assistant for some help cutting some large block letters out of posterboard to spell *PEACE*. After a large-group charting activity in which we defined and gave examples of peace, I split the children into five groups and gave each group one of the two-foot-tall letters. I instructed them to search through magazines looking for peaceful situations in pictures. When they found these types of pictures, the group members had to agree whether the picture was indeed peaceful. If they agreed, they cut it out and glued it on their large letter. The group members continued to do this until their letter was completely filled to overflowing with peaceful pictures.

After all the groups finished filling their letters, we had an art show and talked about our favorite pictures. At the end of the lesson, I hung the letters on the wall above my desk. Anyone who enters and sees me sitting at my desk always sees "PEACE" above my head. It is a great message to send out these days. This activity can be done with virtually any of the character education traits your school emphasizes, such as respect, responsibility, trustworthiness, and, my favorite trait of all, positive attitude. Use your favorite character education traits and create a banner-sized message for your classroom space.

Angela sitting at her desk. Notice the word PEACE above her desk. It serves as a great reminder for today's world.

Having encouraging words and phrases throughout my room has helped me out on those days when I felt a little off balance. The words remind me of my deeper purpose in this life.

Haylee sits in
the thinking area. She holds a soothing oil
and water timer in her hand. Haylee looks in the mirror and tries
to identify her feelings. Perhaps she is sad because she misses her mommy or
because she doesn't want to ride the bus today. Regardless, when she is ready
to come back to the group, she will let the teacher know. The teacher
will say, "I'm so glad you're ready to join us now!"

Thinking Area

Of all the workshops I have attended throughout my years of teaching, my favorite had to do with the success of challenging students. I believe the smart Matthews and the brilliant Adeles will generally do fine in this world of ours, with or without my teaching expertise. Secretly, I always look for the underdog to overachieve. It always seems better than any Hollywood movie to have someone whom most consider an underachiever to come out more successful than anyone would ever have dreamed. Because of this hope, I have made a conscious effort to help improve the lives of the struggling underdogs who enter my classroom year after year.

Throughout my years of teaching, I have noticed that many of these children could not identify their feelings, let alone understand them. They may have felt frustrated or angry, agitated or wound up. Instead of naming those feelings, working through them, and coming out on the other side into a more positive frame of mind, they acted out.

During one particular workshop I attended to learn about helping challenging students, the presenter offered the participants the idea of creating an "angry space" or an "angry area" in the classroom. It was a place where children could stomp and be immersed in their anger. Then upon releasing their feelings, they could return to the group. As a therapist in training, I liked the idea of a therapeutic setting. Because I worked in a public school system, though, I thought I should modify it for the educational world. I believed I could accomplish the same objective by creating a thinking space or area in a corner of my classroom. It would be similar in nature in that the children could go there to identify their feelings. Basically it acts as a small time-out space where the children can gather their emotions. They are able to get back on the positive track where they need to focus on their tasks. For my thinking area, I made sure students knew they were able to go there at any time during the day when they were not quite sure how they were feeling. I did not allow the children to hit or stomp anything. Rather, I provided some anxiety-relieving squeeze balls and a teddy bear to hug as well.

In my classroom, the thinking area is a cozy space with comfy chairs surrounded by posters with emotion-related themes. I've included a mirror for the children to look into for comparing their

Nigel and Kambree sit in the thinking area to discuss how to show respect to friends. On occasion, the teacher may use the thinking area as a space where children can go to discuss any conflict issues they may be having.

images to the faces on the posters. The posters contain a wide array of "feeling" faces, from disappointed to excited. I hang inspirational posters in this area as well. A picture of a puppy that looks sad reads, "I need a hug." Children who feel stressed and angry can use the squeeze balls. Also in the thinking area are oil and water timers and sand timers. They tend to be soothing to look at when our sad and discouraged feelings appear.

The thinking area helps children identify their feelings and move through them. Children are able to go to the thinking area at times of their choosing, or when the teacher needs them to go there after several warnings about misbehavior. The visual posters, soothing timers, inspirational words, and comfy furniture all help students get back into a more balanced state. The area is used as a tool to help them understand their latest emotions. By simply recognizing and acknowledging their feelings, the children move toward becoming emotionally balanced. When children are ready to leave the thinking area and return to the group, they usually return refreshed and ready to begin anew. Many parents and teachers who visit my room often comment that they would love to go reflect in the thinking area. I always have the same response: "You should make your own thinking area at home! Everyone deserves one!"

• • •

These ideas have proved to be very helpful in the school setting. Visually my classroom is bursting with the message "Love This Life!" In this era of teaching, when the world feels irrational and off balance, it is crucial that we remain positive, hopeful, and at peace with the world around us. As we develop these traits for ourselves, we teach the fundamentals of balance to the children who urgently need these types of role models in their lives.

4

Embrace the Clarity of Orderliness

We can do no great things, only small things with great love.
—Mother Teresa, 1910–97, Albanian nun, missionary

We are not able to prepare for all things. Nevertheless, many things we can prepare for, such as meals, our agenda for the day, and appointments. The spontaneous words and actions that occur at these activities we cannot prepare for. Another thing we are unable to prepare for is the amount of stress that is put on each and every one of us today. Teachers in particular have enormous amounts of stress put on them. By being prepared, though, teachers can alleviate the daily stress and tensions they are asked to endure.

While I was writing this book, a colleague and friend said to me, "Angela, I do not know how you do all the things you do." In our discussion, she talked about how I create all the interesting activities for my classroom, take care of my family and home, cook nutritious meals, teach yoga several times a week, facilitate and attend my monthly drama group, exercise daily, and, to top it all off, have a positive attitude to beat the band. I recall explaining my to-do lists, my time-saving ideas, and all the ways I remain balanced as a whole person. I also clarified that I have my "moments" as well, just as everyone does, but for the most part I have developed a system that helps my life flow smoothly. This is how I developed "The Clarity of Orderliness." I realized that by preparing my days, as much as one can prepare a day, my life flows more effectively. This helps me become more conscious of the wonderful moments in the day, leaving more time for spontaneity and creativity. On the other hand, I notice that when I do not prepare my days, I end up more exhausted, impatient, frenzied, and stressed.

Ideas for the Classroom

Here are some ideas that have made my teaching and my life outside of my career flow more efficiently. All of these techniques provide orderliness and efficiency, which in turn help my whole self to feel more balanced and at ease.

Lesson Plans

My lesson plans are quite typical. I do not do anything magical with them, except to make the process more efficient by creating them for a two-week period. This gives me many days of breathing room in my schedule. I create my lessons on the computer because any premade plan book I have ever bought was not quite what I had in mind. So I made my own. I have one sheet for each day of the week. Each day begins with arrival and ends with dismissal. Many things on each day are the same, such as lunch, recess, and morning message. I also change the special classes my students have each day, such as gym, music, and art. I leave blank spots to write in my activities for English-language arts (ELA), math, social studies, and science. I create lessons based on themes that run concurrently in each subject area. And I overplan for each subject. If a lesson is not going quite as planned, I fall back on plan B. Plan B is always short, concise, and available to prevent chaos and added stress. I leave the last Friday of each two-week period open. As I stated, I always overplan, so any extra activity or unused idea is saved for this day. I always make Fridays extrafun. This creates a celebratory atmosphere, which adds a nice touch to the emotional and occupational dimensions of the self.

Folders

I started using folders just a few years ago. They have helped me fine-tune my system even more effectively. As I stated earlier, I create lessons for a two-week period of time. That results in ten lessons, one for each day of the week, times two weeks. For each day within my two-week theme, I create a folder, so I have ten folders per theme. On the front of each folder I attach a laminated generic daily schedule. This helps in case a substitute teacher becomes necessary. Inside the folder is my lesson plan, any books I am reading for the day, and my ELA, math, science, and social studies items. If the items are too big for the folder, I place them on a tray for that particular day. A simple sticky note on the outside of the folder lists all the materials I will need for the day. Bus lists are copied at the beginning of the year, and I put one in each folder. As I gather all my supplies, I cross off the sticky note that I have put on my tray or in my folder.

Developing and using these types of organization and preparation aids will help alleviate any added stress that may come your way throughout the day, thus creating balance for your emotional and occupational aspects of self.

To-Do Lists

My classroom to-do list is a simple paper that has check boxes next to each item. It is taped to my desk so I can refer to it whenever I need to. Anything that needs to be done for the day, week, or term goes on this paper. As I finish each item, I check its box. This helps me build a sense of accomplishment. I list things in order of importance. I label the top five urgent things that need to be done with numbers 1 through 5. This prevents me from rereading the list over and over. Each day I begin with number 1. At times, other, more urgent issues arise and need attention. Those things go on the list and override all other matters. Instead of numbering the item, I draw a star next to it.

For those people who make lists and lose them, it is best to tape the list where you can refer to it easily, for example, to your desk. To-do lists are very helpful. I once attended a workshop for stress reduction. The instructor explained that by simply writing down what stresses you out, you alleviate 10 percent of your stress. By making a to-do list that works for you and helps you prepare your days, you can relieve constant worry, nervous tension, and anxiety. This alone helps balance the emotional self.

Generic Substitute-Teacher Folder

By creating a generic substitute-teacher folder and placing it in clear view somewhere on your desk, you are prepared in case an emergency arises and you need to be away from your classroom. This allows you to first take care of the crisis at hand and not have needless worry about your classroom. I created a generic substitute-teacher folder because of an unforeseen crisis that happened to me years ago. I was six weeks pregnant and my mom died unexpectedly. I was also the executor of her will, so, not surprisingly, I had a lot on my shoulders. Emotionally, I was grieving my loss, and physically, my body was working hard on developing a healthy baby. Needless to say, I did not want to lose sleep about how my substitute was going to survive in my classroom. Because I was not prepared for this, and because I needed extended time off to take care of my mother's estate, I had to take care of my substitute as well. Every day or so I would check in and share with her whom she could ask for help, where supplies were, and what she should be working on with my students. This is how my generic substitute-teacher folder idea was created.

Included in this folder are a list of where things are in the classroom, student helpers, and ideas to save the day. Here are some other materials to include in the generic substitute folder:

- Marking period objectives
- Report cards, benchmarks, and any other paperwork to be done quarterly
- Monday through Friday nonspecific and standard lesson plans that include your daily special classes, such as physical education, art, or music
- Attendance and dismissal procedures
- Where to find lesson plans (including last year's book)
- Lunch tickets
- School schedule and rules
- Class rules and routines
- Seating chart
- Bus lists
- Emergency information, such as fire drills, children with allergies, and confidential custody information
- Anything else you think will be helpful

Compiling this information into a folder does not take long. On the other hand, it would take a lot of time and energy to explain all this information over the phone to someone who does not know your room. This is why such a folder is important to have. The generic substitute-teacher folder is insurance for your peace of mind.

Extra Ideas Folder

As I stated earlier, I find it better to overplan than underplan lessons. One "downside" to overplanning is that I tend to have extra lessons, information, worksheets, and ideas. This is where the extra ideas folder comes in handy. I gather all the extra material that I did not use previously and put it in a file labeled "Extra Ideas." After two months,

I have enough information and activities to put together a "Review" theme for a week. Reviewing for students is helpful, and, furthermore, it helps me not to waste these ideas by throwing them in the recycling bin. I put any sheets that are left over after the review unit into the writing center basket. These ideas become opportunities for extra credit. The children can work on these, if they choose, during a student-initiated center (station) time.

The Extra Ideas folder helps me keep clutter at bay, which has been emotionally and occupationally therapeutic. Spiritually, it helps me feel as though I contributed to saving part of a tree by not simply throwing out unused papers. Instead, the students use the ideas in their learning.

Weekly Newsletters

After I write my lesson plans, I create my weekly newsletter. I do this so I can take the highlights from the weekly lessons and put them into my parent newsletter. This way I hold myself accountable for those specific activities. It would be impossible to include every activity and learning objective in a simple newsletter for parents; therefore, I draw attention to the most important items for the week.

My newsletter is divided into six sections: the theme of study, ELA information, science, math, social studies, and a special news section. The special news section is a wonderful time-saving idea. For instance, if you have several parents who have not returned their child's report card envelopes, you can write in this section that report card envelopes need to be returned by a certain date. When you send home papers, including the newsletter, read this section to the children who need their report card envelopes returned. Ask them for their help. Explain that you need them to read this special news section to their parents. Tell them they will receive a treat if they bring back their envelopes. A simple hand stamp, sticker, or hug will do. This can save you time by alleviating five to six phone calls during the week. So a weekly newsletter can help you stay on track and focused. And reading it to all the children and asking them to share it with their parents helps the children become responsible and accountable young people. By teaching these fundamental life skills, you are instilling worthy values in each child's whole self.

To Be Copied and To Be Filed Folders

Assistants and volunteers come into my classroom to help. Often when they first enter the room, I am busy with whole-group instruction or a quick activity that needs my direct attention. Instead of having my assistants wait for me to finish, I have a To Be Copied folder and a To Be Filed folder. The assistants and other helpers know where to find these folders. Whenever they have a few spare minutes, they look in these folders and help out with these tasks. Of course, if I have a spare minute, I pull these folders and take care of this work as well. Spare minutes here and there add up to precious hours throughout the year. By taking advantage of these free times, you will alleviate the stress associated with piles of endless tasks. This strategy can give you added energy, which helps to balance the occupational and emotional self.

Classroom Flow Layout

The language-rich classroom, the visually inspirational haven, and the classroom flow layout go together like cake and icing. Classroom flow layout simply means arranging the classroom design so the flow within it is smooth. The children's energy can be channeled through the design. By having such a layout, teachers prevent negative behavior and promote ongoing learning. The classroom layout should be straightforward, well thought out, and organized. It should be linear, easy to move through, efficient, and uncluttered.

Included in the layout should be a literacy area, calculation or math center, discovery corner, classroom library, and manipulatives zone. Each labeled center should include clear, concise directions and should relate to the theme at hand. The centers should include inspirationally rich words (see chapter 3's "Visual Cues" section). Students should be able to work independently in these areas of the room. After students finish their required work, they should be able to move freely from one center to another. This freedom allows them to continue with their learning at their own paces.

This type of layout supports student-initiated choices versus only teacher-directed activities (see chapter 7's "Making Choices" section). Students stay on task more easily with these centers, because it is where they choose to occupy their time. Students have fabulous ideas for these areas and enjoy helping create them as well. Although these centers take some time to construct, they help children in many ways. Classroom flow layout enhances a child's intellectual and occupational self. This type of classroom prepares children for making choices in life, a fundamental skill. It further develops their creative and social dimensions as well. By preparing these thematic centers, teachers can minimize students' off-task behaviors.

• • •

Preparation not only alleviates stress, it also helps your life flow more effectively. By being prepared, your mind is calm and can focus more easily. As a result, you have more time for the present moment. I also take time to prepare for the next workday at home. Each night, I lay out the clothes I am going to wear the next day. All lunches are packed. My daughter's diaper bag is geared up, and my son's school agenda is signed and ready. All this preparation allows us a more peaceful morning and helps me begin my workday emotionally ready. Taking time to prepare important aspects of your career and home life will create balance for your emotional health, leaving you less ex-hausted and frenzied, and more creative and energetic.

5

Nurture the Whole Student

Do not go where the path may lead; go instead where there is no path and leave a trail.
—Ralph Waldo Emerson, 1803–82, American poet, philosopher

You've studied the six dimensions of your whole self, shifted your energy to a positive state of being, and found many ways to organize yourself and make your classroom a haven of inspiration. Now you're ready to direct your efforts outward, into helping our world be even more balanced. It is time to turn toward educating your students, our next generation, about the benefits of balance—this is our hope for tomorrow's world.

We as a society must guide our children on the path to knowing. We are living in a world that bombards our youngsters with name brands and images of perfection so unbelievable that even perfect-ten supermodels would have a difficult time living up to these superficial ideals. "If you wear this, you are somebody" and "If you look like perfection, then you are worthy" are the messages being sent to our young people. Our youth are inundated with status issues, and when drugs, alcohol, hormones, and a sensationalized media are added to their quest, an identity crisis, or worse, a disaster, is waiting to happen.

Furthermore, today's school systems seem to be focusing more and more only on the intellectual, or academic, child. The system puts the emotional and physical aspects of children in the background. With the scrutiny of the public school report card and the results of state-wide English-language arts (ELA) and other subject exams that teachers have prepared for and taught during the entire school year, the social, emotional, and occupational dimensions of students do not seem addressed anymore either.

This type of schoolwide reaction sends our children way off kilter, and it is imperative that we as a society examine it. We need to look at our big picture: the school violence, the rise of student suicide, all of today's problems that exist within our young population. When we do this and understand the need for vital change, we will be on a better path going in the best direction, guiding our children in a more holistic and balanced way. We will be concentrating more on the whole child—the spiritual, emotional, physical, social, intellectual, and occupational student.

Watching children uncover who they are is a remarkable process. It is incredible to see them grow into their talents and discover how to honor their gifts. To view these individuals as they support their whole selves is a delight for the balanced teacher. This is the prescription for a better tomorrow: the world shining with people who are using their talents wisely for a healthier life.

When you have a deeper understanding of your own values and you know who you are, it is important that you teach youngsters to understand their whole selves. I believe it is our mission to instill in our children the core values of the collective world, such as respect, honor, and responsibility. This chapter includes exercises you may need to adapt to appropriately meet the age level of the children you work with.

I would like you, as the teacher of balance, to take a moment to reflect on the types of learners in your classroom. Perhaps you are working with very young children. For the most part, these little ones tend to be kinetic learners. Most children at the elementary level will benefit from movement too. As children grow and advance, they are able to adapt to many learning styles, such as visual, audio, and tactile. To keep things simple, I do not provide exercises for every learning style. Instead, I have provided kinetic and visual ideas to meet a range of needs for early elementary to upper middle and high school students. Of course, feel free to modify any of the exercises to meet your classroom's specific needs.

• EXERCISE •

The Whole Self: Identifying the Six Dimensions

Have students place six chairs in a straight line in the front of the room facing the group. Label each chair with one of the dimensions of the whole self. For the first chair, write "Creative Self" on a piece of paper and tape it to the chair. (As I mentioned in chapter 1, although *creative self* refers to the *spiritual self,* when you work in a public school system, the creative self is the more acceptable term to use when working with children.) On the second chair, tape the label for the physical self. The third chair will have the label for the emotional self, and so on. Have the students identify each aspect: creative, physical, emotional, social, intellectual, and occupational.

Explain to the children that we need all six dimensions to make up the whole self. Divide the children into six groups, one group for each dimension, and have each group stand behind a chair and help identify that particular dimension they are working on in their group. As the teacher directs this exercise, she will lend a hand in defining these words. For instance, as a small group of students stands behind the chair labeled "Creative Self," explain that this is where your imagination, excitement, creativity, and passions dwell. Now ask the children to provide some examples of their creative activities. Choose another group of students to stand behind the second chair and discuss the emotional dimension, mentioning a full array of feelings, including happy, sad, angry, and excited. Allow the children to share about these types of expressions. At the "Physical Self" chair, describe this dimension as encompassing healthy habits regarding sleep, exercise, and eating. Let the children discuss some of their healthy behaviors within this particular dimension.

Next, encourage the small group behind the social dimension chair to use such words as *group, community,* and *cooperation* when sharing what they know about the social aspect. For the intellectual dimension, refer to academics, learning, and school. Encourage the children to discuss what's involved in this aspect of their lives. Lastly, identify the occupational aspect as how one occupies time. And, yes, even young children will understand the term *occupational self.* They will be able to give you all sorts of wonderful answers if you simply ask them what they like to do with their time.

Remember to keep definitions simple, especially for younger students. After everyone has shared, use their words to identify, define, and provide examples of each dimension. Your job is to guide and draw out their responses as you continue through each dimension. Once again, the objective is to help students grasp an understanding of each aspect. Be sure to close the lesson by reiterating that the whole self is made up of six complete dimensions.

● **EXERCISE** ●

The Whole Self: Sizing the Six Pie Slices

Have students draw a large circle and divide it into six equal pieces. Basically, they are creating a six-slice pie, making sure every slice is the same size. Tell them to write one dimension of the self in each pie slice: creative, physical, emotional, social, intellectual, and occupational. Explain to older students that if they were completely balanced, this is how their whole self would look. Each pie slice would be precisely equal if a person were ideally balanced in all six dimensions.

Now ask students to identify their strongest area within the pie chart. Ask which dimension is their most powerful strength or their gifted area. The artists in your class may choose their creative self as the strongest section. Those who are extroverted may choose their social dimension, and those who are athletic may choose their physical self as their greatest strength. You get the picture. Have each child put a star next to his or her dimension of greatest strength.

Now ask students to identify a dimension they could improve upon. Then have them redraw their six-slice pie to clearly represent their whole self as they see it. Larger pie slices will represent those aspects that are their strengths. Smaller slices will represent those dimensions that may need some assistance or improvement. Note how the pie slices are no longer identical. Ask students to write a paragraph about one way they could make their whole self more balanced and thus make the pie slices more equal.

• • •

Understanding the Creative Dimension

As I stated earlier, when referring to the spiritual dimension, using the term *creative self* is more acceptable in the public school system, and whatever we create from our hearts in this life, of course, stems from the spirit. We are all here to share our creative selves with the world. We are all undeniably on a divine mission with the responsibility to make the world a healthier place. The universe is eager to have us be our true selves and use the talents we've been given.

We need to teach our youngsters to explore their uniqueness and discover the gifts inside them. By the time children are seven years old, their talents have already been subdued and they have been made to conform to fit into our schoolwide system and today's unbalanced societal makeup. We must help each child uncover his or her individuality. In doing so, we as teachers are genuinely and without a doubt giving to the world in the way we were meant to do.

The objective in teaching children about the creative self is to assist them in uncovering their true talents to benefit the world. By helping them live up to their fullest potential, we all become creatively and spiritually balanced. Included next are exercises to help even the most skeptical student reveal his or her true nature.

The Creative Dimension: Inventing Your Helpful Person

For this exercise, you will need some props. Include several miscellaneous items, such as old shirts, pants, skirts, shoes, and purses, in a box. If you are able to find them, add wigs, hats, scarves, and anything else that looks interesting or useful, plus pencils and paper, to the dress-up box. Explain to the children that today they will be dressing up to create people who will help change the world for the better. They will invent these people by putting on clothes and using the props that are provided. Each child should also give his person a name and identify how that newly invented character is going to help the world we live in.

After everyone has dressed as an invented person, begin an interview process. Basically, try to draw out from the students what makes their characters unique, and what gifts their characters hold. Ask each student questions, making sure the student replies using first-person terminology. For example, if you ask the character, "What is your name?" the student should reply, "My name is . . ." Some other important questions to ask their creations include "What is the most important thing about you?" and "How can you help our world?" By keeping the questions open-ended, you are able to draw out children's creative and higher levels of thinking.

Younger children love to listen to these interviews. Once someone has become a newly invented character, all the children's imaginations become immersed in the dialogue. If you are using this exercise with older students, allow them to do the interviewing and later report their findings to the entire group.

I must remind you that this exercise is about being spontaneous and trusting the process. I assure you that all sorts of interesting and subconscious information will emerge. The teacher's responsibility is to honor, acknowledge, and praise each student's creativity. The underlying objective is to facilitate the activity as the children emerge more fully into their creative selves.

● EXERCISE ●

The Creative Dimension: Four Talents for a Better World

As children grow older, it is fundamentally important to get them thinking about their contributions to the world. In schools, we should ask students this question more often: "What do you want to create in this lifetime?" No one ever asked me this. Instead, the daily grind went into motion and that was the focus. We have been taught to set aside our passions and concentrate on surviving. To transform this way of thinking, first we need to help students uncover their talents and honor their passions. I have heard my psychodrama mentor and others say, "Do what you love and the success will follow." This needs to be the new motto for the creation of a balanced world.

For this visual learning exercise, ask students to draw a stick figure in the center of a piece of paper. This will represent the creative self. Now ask them to fold the paper in quarters so that, when the paper is reopened, the creases form four sections. Have the students identify four of their talents by writing one talent in each section of the paper. Next ask the children to write about how each of their talents will make the world a better place. For example, if one child listed cooking as a talent, perhaps the child would say that the dinners he makes allow people to enjoy food. If a child listed the talent of painting, the child might explain that the world is a brighter place because of her beautiful paintings. It is important to note that every talent expressed provides a benefit. The objective is to honor the talents and to instill in children the wisdom that all talents are valuable.

● ● ●

Understanding the Emotional Dimension

The two hundred emotions we can feel are simply feelings, and it is okay for us to feel them. For many of us, this was not the message we heard growing up. And I would bet the challenging students in your classroom are not given permission to feel much of anything. This is why they act out so much. The messages they hear sound something like this: "If you cry anymore, I will really give you something to cry about." To add to the dysfunction, when the child knows, or moreover feels, the family is in crisis, adults in the family will say, "Nothing is wrong; go to sleep." Overall, children's feelings are negated and not validated. By the time they enter school, it is no wonder they have so many problems. They have been warned all along that they should not feel their emotions. Even more detrimental, they have been told that if they do feel anything, it is incorrect. To put it simply, we have our work cut out for us if we are going to undo this transgression.

Looking back, I wished I had learned the acronym HALT when I was younger. It is a simple concept for when you are feeling out of sorts, and, furthermore, it is a fine place to start addressing the emotional dimension with youngsters. Actually, I learned about HALT from the adults I was working with in therapy and recovery groups. HALT is basically a relapse preventive in addiction recovery. Addicts continually use it to gauge their distance from relapse in recovery and to appraise their daily state of mind. I see it as a fundamental skill to use with all human beings. HALT means to simply stop, or instruct yourself to halt, and then ask yourself, "Am I hungry, angry, lonely, or tired?"

If I sense students are hyperactive and agitated, I will simply say, "Halt," and they will usually respond by saying what is bothering them. I also have the thinking area in my room, which I described in more detail in chapter 3, "Create a Classroom Haven." The area includes a mirror, a squeeze ball, soothing oil and water timers, and a "How are you feeling?" poster. It is a place in the room where the children can go at any point during the day to identify what they are feeling. Recognizing that our emotions change within the course of a day—and what is causing them to change—is a basic life skill you should introduce to students. These next exercises should help you assist your kinetic and visual learners to identify their emotions and find their emotional balance.

The Emotional Dimension: Creating Feelings Posters

In your room, hang posters that depict different emotions. Choose posters that keep the message simple and that each include only one feeling word. Post five to six of these emotion, or "feeling," posters in the room to cover, for example, happy, sad, mad, shy, excited, and scared. Have the students look through magazines and cut out pictures that depict those feelings. Let the students move about freely, gluing pictures on the correct poster. After the posters are finished, divide the children into groups, with one group for each feeling poster. Have each group identify, define, and share examples of their feeling poster. Allow the groups to identify and pantomime the emotion described in their poster. Continue through each group until all students have had a chance to portray their posters.

Afterward, discuss the importance of identifying feelings. Ultimately, convey the worth of sharing our feelings with others. Suggest the children write or draw about emotions in individual "feelings journals."

The Emotional Dimension: Graphing Our Weekly Emotions

Recognizing why our emotions change within the course of a day is a basic life skill you should introduce to children. Make a classroom feelings chart and title it "Our Classroom Feelings." For younger children, draw some faces showing basic emotions at the top of the page to help the children begin to identify feelings. Write the days of the week across the top of the chart and the children's names along the side. During group time, ask each child to identify how she is feeling today. Document the children's responses next to their names under that day of the week. Ask them to recognize possible reasons for their feelings. They may not know at that particular time, and that is okay. Continue with the feelings chart for two weeks. Afterward, as a group, review the charts to note any patterns, changes, and interesting features. You can begin this by simply asking the students, "What do you notice?" From this point, you can turn your chart into a math lesson by graphing and documenting the information obtained during the two-week period.

• • •

Understanding the Physical Dimension

When I think of becoming a physically balanced person, I immediately think of becoming physically fit. But there is more to the physically balanced person than simply exercising to look toned. To be a balanced person in the physical dimension, we need to look at both a person's inside and outside physical components. One can look physically fit but be unhealthy internally. It is critical to teach our youngsters about both the internal and the external parts of becoming a physically balanced person. We can teach them how to tune in to their inner self as well as their outer part.

Our society is flooded with images of the picture-perfect body. These images are undoubtedly too much to live up to. The impressions they leave, though, can lead us to feelings of unworthiness, self-doubt, and depression. It is vital that we teach our youngsters how to honor their own body's wisdom. In doing this, we teach them how to take back their power and give less and less attention to unrealistic picture-perfect images.

The outer physical dimension is usually quite clear cut to understand. Are you overweight or underweight? Is your body overall toned, or could you use some help in that area? We live in a society in which the majority of people are overweight. I recall reading the back of a cereal box one morning at breakfast. It stated that two-thirds of people in the United States are over a healthy body fat ratio. I realized that everywhere I looked, the local and national news included health alerts about this issue. Even the news station on my way to work highlights America's latest problem, obesity. My monthly yoga readings and other health-filled magazines include front cover stories about the newest and fastest way to lose all this weight. Obviously obesity is an issue here in the United States. More important, we need to educate our youngsters that quick-fix weight-control solutions, such as fad diets and pills, are not the way to go. Instead, teach them that if they are overweight, it is important to go back to the basic fact that if they move more and eat less, they will lose weight. For most people, it is that simple!

Personally, I feel physically balanced most of the time. To keep my outer and inner physical selves balanced, I have developed the habit of checking in with myself every so often. I ask myself, "How I am doing physically?" And, on occasion, my body responds, "Drink more water" or "Get to bed early tonight; you're tired!" It is important that we also teach our children how to tune in to their inner physical selves.

By its nature, internal physical health is more difficult to explain to children. For that reason, our awareness and the teaching of it are more important than ever these days. The internal physical dimension has to do with listening to the messages your body sends you. Listening to your body is a remarkable skill, especially when we live in the middle of a world in which it is becoming more challenging to find your peaceful inner voice.

First, you must understand the fundamentals of the internal physical component. Our body needs plenty of water over the course of the day. It needs ample amounts of rest, relaxation, and nourishment.

Moreover, it is important that we learn to listen to our body's messages. We need to teach our youngsters how to listen to and seek advice from these internal messages.

For example, if you are sick, your body will let you know. It may let you know on the first day with the beginnings of a scratchy throat. If you do not listen to it and honor its wisdom, the next message could come through as congestion. And, if you do not listen to that message, your body may possibly tell you next about chest pains and exhaustion. This will continue until you cannot ignore the warnings any longer and are sick with a cold, the flu, perhaps eventually pneumonia, or something else debilitating. Looking back, if you had listened to the first message and stayed home and drunk hot tea and nurtured yourself, you may have avoided the more unbearable conditions.

Once again, teaching our youngsters to tune in to their internal physical dimension, as well as their outer physical self, is a required skill for maintaining physical balance. Before beginning the following exercises, ask children to close their eyes and listen to their breaths. Use a serene voice as you ask them to feel their breaths going in and out. Creating a bit of awareness about the physical self always helps focus the students. The two exercises are for kinetic and visual learners on becoming a more physically balanced person. You may need to modify them to meet the children's needs. For instance, if children are not reading yet, use picture cues to help them understand your topic.

● EXERCISE ●

The Physical Dimension:
Understanding Physical Balance

Ask your students, "What does it mean to be physical?" Many youngsters enjoy going to gym. Talk about the words *physical education*. Break each word down. Having the physical education teacher come in to talk with the children would also be a good idea. She could share exactly what it means to teach physical education to youngsters. Then use this simple yet effective way to bring to light some understanding of physical balance.

Have the students put one hand on their heart and feel their normal heartbeat. Have them put both hands on their cheeks to feel their normal temperature. Next have the students jog in place, do jumping jacks, and other forms of exercise. Afterward, have the children again put a hand over their heart to feel the heartbeat. Ask them to feel their face again and notice their body temperature. Ask the students, "If your body could talk, what is it saying to you?" Serve water and a healthy food at snacktime and continue to discuss the body and its messages.

This works for older students as well. In today's unbalanced world, it is always good to be refreshed with some of the basics. Be sure not to forget the aspects of drinking ample water, getting enough rest, following healthy diets, and exercising. To wrap up the exercise, ask the children to break into groups and share with each other what it means to be physically balanced. With younger children, you may need to discuss the word *balance* and give them some examples of it, such as a balance beam, a weight balance, or a teeter-totter. Ask each group to suggest one way they could become more physically balanced.

• EXERCISE •

The Physical Dimension: Charting Physical Balance

This simple exercise works well for both younger and older children, although with younger children, you may want to include little stick-figure drawings along with the words. Write "Physically Balanced" in the center of a piece of chart paper. Draw a circle around the words. Now divide the chart paper into four sections: top left, top right, bottom left, and bottom right. Make sure the "Physically Balanced" circle touches all four segments. The list in each segment will overlap with the circle, showing how all four segments contribute to being physically balanced.

In the first segment, write "Exercise." Brainstorm with the students all the ways we exercise, including fun ways, such as watertubing, in-line skating, and other activities. In the next section, write "Healthy Eating Habits." Devise a list of how to eat well, indicating the types of foods, how much, and types of drinks, such as water, mineral and vitamin drinks, milk, and juices. In the third area, write "Rest and Relaxation." Create a list there that states how much rest is appropriate and why rest is important. List various activities for leisure. You will most likely want to emphasize the moderation of video games and television in this segment. In the fourth section, write "Messages from Your Body." Brainstorm the messages the body gives us on a daily basis. After each point, describe how to appropriately respond to those messages.

After the chart has been completed, ask the students to share with a friend what it means to be physically balanced. Ask them also to share one way they could improve upon their physical self.

• • •

Understanding the Social Dimension

It is interesting to me that of all the dimensions of the whole self, people usually think students grasp the social dimension best. Whether that's true or not, it is the area where major transformation needs to take place for our youngsters. Too many cliques and far too many judgments are already formed by the time children are in second grade. By middle school, rivalries are occurring between groups. And high school offers fewer opportunities for positive connections between cliques. Gangs are sometimes formed at this level.

Schools need to be educating children about these issues at a very young age. Use age-appropriate language for young children when discussing these matters, of course. Mention that it is not okay to shun others. Role-play rejections. Discuss feelings. Review this important topic often. Proactively heading off these harmful mind-sets is the greatest strategy the balanced teacher uses.

For ethical equilibrium within our future social order, it is critical for our children to be balanced in this area. When educating students about the social dimension, we need to guide them into shared mutual living for their happiness and that of others. These are essential things children need to learn. The next exercises entail movement and visual perception of the dynamics of the social self. The objective is that students will obtain a deeper understanding of their social selves.

• EXERCISE •

The Social Dimension: Choose a Fascinating Person

Have the students stand in a circle. Instruct them to look around at all the others and think about what they find fascinating about each person. This is done silently. Next have them put their right hand on the shoulder of a classmate they find interesting and would like to know more about. They are only allowed to choose one person. After everyone has put a hand on the shoulder of a classmate, note aloud any interesting observations. For example, "I notice Kurtis was selected by five people." Beginning with Kurtis, ask the students to explain why they picked him. One might say, for example, "I chose you, Kurtis, because I find [the aspect or reason] interesting and would like to know more." Make sure the child is looking at the selected person, not at you, while explaining why. This confirms ownership of the selection. Keep moving along until each child has told his selected person what about that person is fascinating.

After all children have had a chance to explain their choice, ask whether anyone did not get selected, noticing if any child does not have a hand on her shoulder. Have those children step aside and think of one interesting thing about themselves they could share with the class. Have them write this on a piece of paper and put it in a hat. Next, while the entire class sits in a circle, pull one piece of paper from the hat at a time and have the class guess which student wrote it. This will help those students who did not get chosen feel important and powerful as well.

• EXERCISE •

The Social Dimension: Similarities among Social Groups

This exercise is not only visual but also kinetic. On a piece of large chart paper write "Social Groups." Ask the children to identify all the social groups they can name, for example, athletes, artists, and intellectuals. Record the children's responses on the chart paper. Next, write each group identity on a separate piece of paper and place it in a separate area in the classroom. For example, write "Athletes" on a piece of paper and put it in one corner of the room. Write "Artists" on another piece of paper and place it somewhere else in the room. When all the words have been distributed around the room, instruct the students to go stand in the area they feel is most like them.

When everyone has selected a social type and moved into that group, instruct the students in each group to write down characteristics about their particular social category. When finished, have each social group bring its characteristics list back to the large group. With the entire class, chart the characteristics next to each classification on the chart paper. Note all the differences but highlight all the similarities. The object is to focus on the connections and note any misunderstandings and preconceptions that may exist about any social group.

• • •

Understanding the Intellectual Dimension

It is critical that we convince our students they do hold wisdom, their minds are sharp, and they can identify the good judgments they need to make. We need to reveal to them the value of studying and contemplating about the world they live in so they can further recognize their place in it. This is vital because this knowledge provides the freedom that will allow their spirits to soar. A person who has great intellectual ability is able to think profoundly and reason in an intelligent and exceptional way. Below are exercises for preschool-age children to adults. And, yes, even preschool children have the knack of sharing their intellectual expertise.

● EXERCISE ●

The Intellectual Dimension: Sharing Talents

Divide the students into groups with a maximum of five children to a group. Beforehand, explain that each person in the group is to identify something he does really well. Afterward, have each group select one of the given skills to learn about. The child whose skill was chosen will teach the group about it. For example, in one group, perhaps a student said she was good at performing bike stunts, another told about cooking, another child spoke about reading skills, and another shared about drawing ability. Now the group will need to pick one of the talents to learn about. If the children have access to the Internet, almost any degree of study is possible. For example, if they choose bike stunts, the student who said she is good at it needs to explain how and why. She can share how long she has been practicing her skill. She can describe the characteristics of a bike stunt rider and so on. Next she can teach about the basic skills you need to have before you can actually perform incredible bike stunts. Items of study could include practicing bike maintenance, riding in a pace line, and following simple stunt safety information. Perhaps showing a video of someone performing bike stunts would be an added highlight. Remind the students that it is not necessary and, moreover, not important that they become an expert at this skill too. Instead, gaining understanding and appreciation of other talents is the objective.

Afterward, come together as a class to discuss all the new fields the students learned about today. Create an honest and giving atmosphere, allowing for free discussion and open feelings. Inquire further about the characteristics of each talent. Are there similarities and differences among those the various groups studied? Be sure to point out how practicing the skill and having a love of it are common elements regarding all the talents. Ask whether the study sparked any new interests.

End this exercise by discussing why it is important to learn about the world we live in. Include ideas about how each of us is able to uncover our own strengths and recognize the talents of others through curiosity and study. An intellectual study not only connects us to the world at large but also helps validate our place within it.

> • **EXERCISE** •

The Intellectual Dimension: Studying Something New

This exercise, or project, will continue for as long as two weeks. It is a group learning technique that will enhance the group's knowledge of a new topic. Furthermore, it will give the students the freedom to explore their intellectual selves. Please note that this exercise can be done with virtually any topic of study.

Day One: Begin by charting the definition of *intellectual*. It should include the thinking and examining we do to understand our world. Afterward, brainstorm all the ways we investigate and study our world. Record all the responses on chart paper. Next, form groups of three to six children. Ask each group to decide on a new topic of study that interests all members. This may take some grasping and groping around at first as students brainstorm and discuss options. Not to worry, though; the cooperative grouping will appear, especially when the children know a time frame is involved. Remind them that they should choose a subject they know little about.

Day Two: As a class, review yesterday's brainstorming efforts. Refer to all the students' responses about how to investigate the world we live in. Some ideas may include reading about the topic, looking it up on the Internet, interviewing an expert about the subject, taking a class, and drawing a picture or diagram. Next, have the students divide into their groups and determine how each group will study its topic. Groups should devise a minimum of three ways to explore their topics of interest.

Days Three and Four: Allow the students to carry out their investigations on their topics. Some children may need to go to the library; others may need access to the computer; others may visit the art department to create illustrations about their studies; and some students may need to do phone interviews or put questions to other workers in the school. Toward the end of Day Four, the students should be compiling all their information and organizing their new knowledge as preparation for how they will display and present it.

Day Five: The children should again divide into their groups to discuss how they will present their newfound knowledge to the class. Have each group practice and prepare its showcase by providing a presentation for the entire class.

Days Six through Nine: Allow each group to present its new intellectual growth. Permit the audience to draw ideas or write questions while the group is presenting. As each group finishes, allow a question-and-answer period. For any questions that go unanswered, ask how we could find out this information.

Day Ten: Ask each group to discuss what it learned. Referring to Day One's brainstorming, ask about the importance of intellectual growth and balance. Chart all the students' responses.

• • •

Understanding the Occupational Dimension

Students do not need to hold a job to understand the occupational self. As I've mentioned, there is much more to the occupational dimension than simply having a job or being employed. Rather, the occupational dimension as I teach about it is concerned with how you occupy your time. What do you do with the moments given to you? How do you engage your attitude within the course of a day? Seeking occupational balance becomes about distributing your time wisely.

Even as I worked on this book, I set a timer for each writing session, because I had many other things that needed my attention. I must do the things that require my time, such as laundry, cleaning, grocery shopping, and bill paying. But I do not allow those things to occupy all my time. I balance things out. I provide myself with plenty of time for what I love to do, including writing, drawing, scrapbooking, playing with my children, cooking, and reading. I give myself many opportunities to explore my passions, relax in my dreams, and discover how else I should use my time.

In the introduction to this book, I mentioned the newest classification used in our schools these days. It is the label many of our youngsters are now forced to carry, Asperger's, which falls under the umbrella of the autism spectrum disorders. One characteristic of Asperger's is that the child being classified tends to exhibit a degree of obsessive-compulsive disorder (OCD). I believe many adults have a bit of this syndrome as well. I further believe that if we teach our children at a very young age how to occupy their time in a balanced manner, many of the symptoms and problems of OCD could be alleviated. Included next are exercises to help children balance their time. Adults may find some encouragement from doing these exercises as well.

• EXERCISE •

The Occupational Dimension: Creating Time for Passions

In a large group, ask students what they like to do with their time. After everyone has responded, choose two or three of the activities the children could do at school, such as drawing or performing music, and ask them how much time they would like to do that particular activity. Explain to the students that as a class they are going to learn about the importance of spending time on the things they love to do.

Having a timer ready, allow the students to do one of their chosen activities. Tell them that when the timer goes off, they should return immediately to the group meeting place. Set the timer for only five minutes and allow them to become involved in their activity. When the children return to the group after the timer has rung, discuss how it felt to have only a few minutes to do what they love.

Next set the timer for twenty minutes. Allow the children to partake in the same activity. When the timer goes off, remind the children to return again to the group and ask them to discuss how each of them felt about this longer amount of time for the activity. Explore the differences of the timed activities, and discuss further why it is important to do the things we enjoy in life. It is critical that we do things we love while here on earth. I have heard it said, "Life is too short"; however, I believe more fully in what I have learned along my path: "life is too long" not to include in it a majority of pleasurable events and the things we love.

• EXERCISE •

The Occupational Dimension: Creating a Balanced Day

The objective of this exercise is to teach children how to balance their days. Later, this will become a weekend assignment for the students. Present this particular activity on a fun Friday afternoon. It is a good way to get the children motivated and busy with worthwhile activities for their upcoming weekend. Begin in the classroom by drawing a picture of a clock with numbers on a piece of chart paper. Title this piece "Using My Time Wisely!" During group time, discuss the term *passion* with the students. Begin by asking the students about their passions. Briefly touch on the word *addiction* as well. I mention this because I know many twelve- and thirteen-year-olds who could be identified as addicted to video games and things of that nature. Ponder this question with the students: "How much time should I spend on my passion?" Some follow-up questions to ask might include "Can you spend too much time on your passions?" and "What do you think happens to a person if he or she spends little or no time on his or her passions?"

Next, break down the day into half-hour increments. These can be written on paper and explained verbally. For all practical purposes, consider this day to be a Saturday. Begin by recording 8 AM and end with 10 PM. As a group, decide how to spend a typical day. For example, some may say they would like to exercise first, but others may want to eat breakfast. Come up with an agreeable schedule for everyone, making sure to include all the basics, such as eating, washing, work, and rest. Make sure the students' favorite activities are also included within the schedule. Record this information on a standard sheet of paper and copy enough for all the students. Ask the children to try to live by this schedule for one day during the weekend.

When the students return to school on Monday, discuss their scheduled day. Ask if they experienced any glitches in the schedule. Discuss how each of them could improve on the schedule. Talk about how they felt at the end of the day. End this lesson with a discussion on the topic of balancing your occupational self.

• • •

It is important to note that once a teacher of balance has a deeper understanding of his or her own self and is aware of all the dimensions he or she needs to care for, helping children comprehend the idea of balance will come more readily. The message is intended for the teacher first, as we discussed in chapter 1. When a person lives a balanced life, he or she is already teaching it on a hidden level. Instructing children directly about balance will not be simply introductory, but, more important, it will be the illuminating experience children need and deserve. The expansion on the topic of balance is absolutely necessary for a more balanced world.

6

Give the Gift of Connection

> *Today, see if you can stretch your heart and expand your love so that it touches not only those to whom you can give it easily, but also those who need it so much.*
>
> —Daphne Rose Kingma, 1942–, inspirational teacher, speaker, and consultant

We are now living in a world in which e-mail, computers, text messaging, cell phones, and the latest technology are seemingly the only ways we communicate with one another. We could conceivably stay in the confines of our homes and never leave or talk directly with anyone. People can run their businesses, pay their bills, accept and decline items of importance over the Internet, and have food, clothing, books, and movies delivered to their front doorsteps. As convenient as this may sound, it is not a healthy way to live. We need to connect with others in a humane way to create a better world for everyone involved.

In this chapter, we'll discuss what it means to connect with others and why we need to do it. Here you will also find ways to positively connect with others. Student activities are provided for making positive connections within the classroom. In addition, you'll gain ideas for teachers to find encouraging ways to connect with our peers, administrators, parents, and the world around us.

I love the way I have heard some inspirational authors discuss the term *connections*. To name the precise author or book would be quite difficult, since I used to be an inspirational author junkie, a fifteen-year addict. I took in every fearless, miracle, sacred, healing, living, yoga-path, self-help nonfiction piece I came across. I highlighted the texts, took notes, pushed books on friends, and taught others too. I meticulously worked it until one day my sister-in-law asked me, "Don't you ever read for fun?" I seriously knew she was right. I slowly weaned myself into a more balanced state. I started by reading inspiring true stories and gradually added some fiction books just for the pleasure of reading. In any case, I am blessed to remember the term *connections* from that excessive time in my life. It stuck with me because I highly admired one author's wordplay with it. I thought it was clever how she discussed people getting off planes or other vehicles to "make a connection." A connection, in this sense, is what a person needs to continue on a journey. I further related when she mentioned how people "have connections," which means they know others who can help them. Connecting means all of these things. I appreciated the idea of connection on this deeper level. To connect means helping one another and joining together for this journey. I realized through these readings that the journey is the whole entity. This is why the idea of connecting was so rousing to me. It completes our social dimension to connect. Our intellectual and spiritual aspects are strengthened as we relate and bond with one another.

The reality, however, is that many of us do not connect with others daily. We go through our days on autopilot, not truly connecting with our children, spouses, friends, or anyone else. We walk the halls at work and say, "Hi, how are you?" and others on autopilot say, "Good. How are you?" When we ask ourselves why we do not take time to sincerely bond with others, we shrug it off and say such things as "Our schedules are too tight," "I wanted to but I just got too busy," and "I have too much to do and will try harder tomorrow."

The truth is that genuine connecting can sometimes be scary. You have to take some risks and you have to learn to trust. Risking and trusting are characteristics of successful people. They are skills that should be taught to our young people; they are skills we should practice as well.

"If I am to die, then how shall I live?" is a question I have posted on my filing cabinet at school, on my refrigerator at home, and in a few other places where I can view it easily. It is there to remind me of how I want to live my life. I want to live free from fear and full of hope. I want to live joyfully and be excited about my work. I want to be free to be me. I am certain that if I died tomorrow, I would not say, "Gosh, am I glad I did not open up and connect with that person." Rather, I would probably wish I had been more genuine, more "me"-like.

It is critical that we all become more genuine and authentic in our day-to-day behavior. The unbalanced world is full of illusions, and we should not add more false impressions to it by not being who we truly are; it is better to simply be our genuine selves. If you surf the television, you'll see that shows and advertisements depict unrealistic bodies, relationships, and behaviors. Typical U.S. magazines paint pictures of perfect situations and people. These are all fabrications with nothing genuine about them. These days, it is more important than ever that we become the authentic and true individuals we are. In doing so, we honor ourselves and balance our spiritual nature.

Included next are ideas that can help you connect more openly, more freely, more like yourself. When you do so, you will strengthen your social self and support your intellectual and emotional dimensions. Remember, it is up to you to free your behavior to be more "you"-like.

Connecting with Others

As a teenager and young adult, I was very self-conscious about connecting with others, especially boys. I would not casually call anyone, let alone a member of the opposite sex, in fear that that person would not want to connect with me. Luckily my mother ingrained in me this idea: "Well, if they don't want to connect with you, it is their loss." She used healthy, positive words to tell me I had a good spirit to connect to. Even today, I still hold her words dear. I take the necessary risks and initiatives to connect with others, to touch base, and to become friends. I highly recommend you do as well. Take the risk to call someone, to visit a friend, to touch base with those you find interesting. It is a rewarding experience to get to know someone. More times than not, you'll find the other person was insecure about connecting with you too. It takes someone to make the first move—why not be the one to make it?

Take a moment to think of other ways you can connect with others, such as sending e-mails, writing notes, and stopping by the classroom. Are there certain people with whom you would like to be closer? What step could you take today to make that happen? What is one thing you could share about yourself to open that connecting door?

Take Five Minutes

Take five minutes in the morning to stop and say hello to others. Ignore the work and do not partake in shoptalk. Instead, make a conscious decision to learn more about other people's lives. Learn what others are passionate about. You'll find an extra five minutes in the course of the day to catch up on the missed work.

Socially Exercise

Exercise with a friend at the end of the workday. Take fifteen or twenty minutes to walk the halls or work out in your classroom. Exercise is essential for your physical and emotional health. When you keep fit with a friend, you show support for one another.

Appreciate Friendships

Think of a person you enjoy being with at work. Write a card telling him how much you appreciate the friendship. Remember that it is okay to take a risk with a feeling or two and share it with the other person.

Share One Nice Thing

At the dinner table with your family, hold hands and share one nice thing about one another before you eat your meal.

Give a Token of Positive Energy

Leave a piece of candy and a small note in someone's mailbox at school. Let the person know you enjoy her positive energy.

Stop and Talk

When someone asks, "How are you?" stop and talk to them. Tell the person two good things that are going on in your life. Then ask about that person's life. Tell the person you want to hear something good.

Offer a Bright Thank-You

If you have an assistant or any volunteers who work in your classroom, give them a candle and attach a note to it thanking them for making your life a little brighter.

Encourage the Interesting Life

Stop in and visit someone you find interesting. Tell the person precisely what you find interesting and encourage the person to continue and do more. Share a little of your philosophy and explain how it connects to that person's viewpoint.

Connecting in the Classroom

At the beginning of the year, I like to use many exercises so the students can make constructive connections with one another. Later in the year, I use those exercises again. I modify them to work on any social difficulties that need to be addressed, such as bullying, shunning, or simply teasing issues. The students can always use some help in re-connecting with one another and understanding who they are. These activities also help children gain a deeper sense of who they are and what they believe in.

● EXERCISE ●

Connecting with Who I Am

This is a simple connecting game that also helps children identify their interests and talents. I recall having to do a similar warm-up exercise in a public relations group once. I modified it by providing movement, along with emotional and physical connection, which makes this exercise well rounded, addressing more of the dimensions of the self. Anytime I use role-playing techniques to their fullest potential, I am using movement and connection as a source of healing.

Give a small piece of tape and paper to each child. Have students write at the top, "Who am I? I am . . ." Instruct them to write the numbers 1 through 5 on the paper, or the numbers 1 through 10 for older children. Next to each number, ask the children to write something about themselves, such as what they are or how they are feeling. For example, a child might write something like this:

Who am I? I am . . .

1. a student.
2. a brother.
3. funny.
4. a good artist.
5. feeling happy today.

Have each child tape the list to his or her chest so others can see it. Next, have the children walk around and silently read all of the lists. Remind students that no one is to comment at this time; they are only to read what others have written. After everyone has read each person's paper, have the group sit in a circle. Ask them to close their eyes and think of one thing they read and to recall who that person was.

Next, ask the group to stand up. Instruct everyone to go to that person they recalled and put their hand on that person's shoulder. At this point, the group somewhat looks like a spider web. Go around and have each child look at the person they selected and now tell why they chose him or her. For example, the teacher would begin by saying, "I noticed Johnny chose Michayla. Johnny, look at Michayla and tell her why you chose her." All hands stay on shoulders until everyone has finished. It is important that the children use "I" words in their statements. For instance, Johnny might say, "I chose you, Michayla, because you wrote that you are the only child who lives in your home." Ask Johnny why that is of interest to him. He may say, "I am the only child who lives in my home too."

You can do this exercise with younger children as well. Ask students to number their papers 1 through 3 and draw their answers instead. They will be able to connect with one another through their drawings.

The important thing with this exercise is to find the connections. Have children expand their answers. Probe and investigate a little more. Ask the students why they found their selections interesting. Have the children look at each other when sharing their answers. Connecting is the key.

• EXERCISE •

Connecting Using the "How Do You Feel?" Scale

This is a fun exercise that teaches youngsters there are almost always two sides to any story. This simple activity requires no materials. You can do it at the beginning of the year to help the children get to know one another better. This exercise can also be done with virtually every theme and subject area imaginable. I originally learned it while obtaining my therapy credits. I recall using a psychodramatic continuum scale in which the participants had to line up in a straight row in accordance with the numbers zero to ten. In other words, the people on the left ranging from zero heading up did not care for a certain topic, and the higher numbers in the straight row approved of or liked that particular topic. In these types of healing groups, most of the topics were more therapeutic-related, such as abuse issues, passive-aggressive problems, and self-esteem troubles. The example provided is actually a modification and more for the educational setting.

Simply ask the children how they feel, on a scale of zero through ten, about a certain topic, idea, or item. To help children learn about each other, for instance, ask them how they feel about country music on a scale of zero through ten. Zero represents extreme dislike; ten represents ultimate love. Next, have the students create a scale, a long continuum with their bodies. They line up in order of how they feel. People who are zeros line up to the left; ones and twos are next; tens are at the far right. When the students are all in line, have them say the numbers they chose regarding country music. You can expand on this activity by having the nines and tens persuade the lower numbers to move higher up the continuum, and the zeros try to draw converts to their view. The key here is to get the children to speak with one another. Here are some topics and ideas you can use for the "How Do You Feel?" scale activity:

- Flying in airplanes
- Dancing
- Math, science, or other subjects
- Specific storybooks or authors
- Rock and roll and other music
- Bike riding, football, tennis, ice-skating, swimming and other sports
- Fall, winter, summer, spring
- Picnics
- Video games

The list is endless. Remember, the goal is to find connections with one another and to begin dialogues among the students. The movement is another key element in this activity. Kinetic flow invokes feelings and creates a warm atmosphere.

• • •

Connecting is an essential aspect of developing the social, emotional, and occupational dimensions of the self. It is necessary that we teach children the importance of connecting with others. Genuine sharing will help them acquire a natural concern for others. It will also help them in developing social friendships that are authentic. All of this makes our world a brighter place.

7

Embark on the Journey Ahead

How wonderful it is that nobody need wait a single moment before starting to improve the world.

—Anne Frank, 1929–45, German-Dutch diarist

Sometimes it only takes a little something to make an enormous impression. This has been true in my life. Several times someone has said a sentence or two that affected my life for the better, helped me move forward in my life. One time, I had to move out of the house I was living in because it had been sold. I had only two weeks or so to find a new home for my two-year-old son and myself. Unfortunately, this was also the time of midterm exams during my sophomore year. I had convinced myself to quit college and reassured myself I would be able to return to my education someday. In the back of my mind I knew that if I quit college, I might never begin again. I told my woes to a friend and she simply said, "What are you doing? You can move fast! Don't quit college. I have seen you move fast!" That friend actually became quite an angel in my life. At the darkest hours in my life, she would say something that would guide me back onto the path where I needed to be. Needless to say, I did move fast. I moved to a new home, settled in, and also completed my schooling over the next few years. I kept moving forward. I moved ahead not just physically but emotionally, intellectually, and occupationally as well. This is why my moving story always stays so close to my heart, because it affected me in so many aspects.

Moving forward and staying on track are important skills in life. Whether you are moving forward physically, emotionally, or whatever, the key is to keep going forward on your journey. The alternative is to stay in a rut and be unproductive and unhappy. We need to remember that even the littlest things we do daily in our teaching influence the lives of children forever. We also need to remember that it is critical we help children move forward, physically, emotionally, and in all other ways.

Children also need to move, literally. They are kinetic people and this is how they learn. Especially when they get stuck emotionally, it is important that we help them advance. Unfortunately, if children are reprimanded for moving around too much or are not helped in moving forward emotionally, they can oftentimes get stuck and diagnosed with some disorder. As we move forward, we need to keep in mind that our youngsters need to move as well. When you provide opportunities for children to move, positive behavior becomes evident and negative behavior diminishes. I believe this is true because children love to play, and movement to children is a type of play. The "moving forward" philosophy is intended for students of all ages; the techniques provided in this chapter should be modified to suit the children you teach. It is critical that we set the precedent and instill the fundamentals of movement for our young children. Included next are exercises that will help us all move forward, and keep moving forward emotionally, physically, and in all areas.

Kinetic Refocusing Techniques

Kinetic refocusing technique is a term I coined when I was explaining to one of my student teachers how to help children get back on task.

It is a simple, quick technique that allows children to play dramatically, yet it redirects them back to the task on hand. You can use it anywhere anytime you feel your students are getting a little restless. You also use these techniques to help all children get back on task and involved and active in their learning.

Kinetic refocusing techniques are quite simply movements that allow students to do something kinetic related to the theme at hand. For example, if you are reading a book and the children are getting a little fidgety, have them do something related to the book. If you are reading a winter story that includes mittens, ask children to pretend to put on their favorite color of mittens. You can also ask them to shake their mittens to the left, then to the right. Have them shake a friend's hand. Then ask them to put their mittens back on their lap while they continue to listen to the story.

Kinetic refocusing techniques are all about being spontaneous. Because very young children are naturally spontaneous and sometimes impulsive, you never know when you will need to pull a little classroom management idea from your sleeve. Kinetic refocusing techniques do just that, plus offer theme-related ideas. Therefore, they serve three purposes. They provide children with movement, relate theme attributes, and provide classroom management to boot.

It is possible to create movement for every activity throughout the day. Another example I often hear problems about is in the hallway. Many teachers will tell me about their students who misbehave while walking in the hallway. There are many ways you can use kinetic refocusing techniques to deal with this problem. For instance, let's say you are doing a theme on bears. Before going in the hallway, tell the students to pretend they are going for a walk in the woods and they need to be extra quiet, for they do not want to scare the bears away. Begin your journey in the hallway by tiptoeing. If students tend to get a little noisy, act surprised and whisper, "Shhh. Did you see the bear over there?" I assure you students will look to where you point and hush because they will want to see the next bear in the forest. Remember to be spontaneous, have fun, and keep the children moving and looking around their world. The objective with kinetic refocusing techniques is to keep the students involved, active, and moving forward!

Older students will benefit from movement as well. When you want children to give you five minutes of their time so you can explain something, use this kinetic refocusing activity that serves as a classroom management strategy. Simply say, "Boys and girls, please give me five," and ask the children to stop and hold up one hand for a moment. It is a simple cue for them to refocus their energy on you. Another attention getter teachers often use is turning out the lights. To add to this, I suggest you have the children briefly cover their eyes so they can clearly refocus and hear your item of importance.

Once again, these are simple kinetic refocusing techniques that help children stay involved and moving forward on their journey.

Memory Button

Frequently in teaching I ask children to "press your memory button." It is the area between your eyebrows. I have often heard it referred to as the third eye or the creative center. When I need children to recall an important piece of information, I will simply say to the entire group, "Okay, everyone, let's talk about respect. Press your memory button." As I press the space between my eyebrows, the children will do the same. I announce, "I know we have talked a great deal about respect in the classroom. I am wondering if anyone can remember our respect rules." As children press their "memory buttons," many hands go up in the air. Movement within the body invokes feelings, and those feelings invoke growth. Growth is essential on the journey ahead. This type of evolving, moving forward, promotes positive development. It is a valuable, effective skill in life balance. Getting children to move as they learn is an exciting way to help them retain important and noteworthy values.

I use the memory button in other ways as well. When I notice a child is stuck trying to answer a certain question, I will simply say,

"Billy, press your memory button to remember." I do this for various reasons. Once again, movement invokes feelings, and once you are able to identify your feelings, you can then explain your actions and ideas more clearly. More times than not, as the child presses the area between the eyebrows, he becomes "unstuck." The answer comes and he can reply confidently. Second, children like to move, as they are lively beings full of energy. A simple touching of the forehead area can also thaw a frozen moment.

Carpet Pieces

Not only do children need to be active, they also need to learn about their personal space in this world. Even the simplest idea or free item can make a world of difference in the classroom. I use carpet remnants throughout the course of my day to help with both active involvement and individual space.

Fortunately for us teachers, sample carpet pieces are abundant. If you go to any flooring store and tell the manager you are a school teacher who could use sample carpet pieces for your classroom (one for each child), the manager will be more than happy to supply you with what you want. I use the carpet pieces in a variety of ways, and I am sure you will come up with other uses.

One strategy is to hand out these remnants as space treats. When you notice good behavior, point it out so the entire class can hear you. Perhaps the class is working on independent reading time, and some children are off task, poking at their friends with their pencils or something of this nature. Simply announce the good child's behavior: "I like the way Sally is reading. Sally, come get a carpet remnant." As a reward, students are able to take those remnants anywhere in the room. They lie on their bellies, their backs, and their sides. They sit crossed legged, and sometimes they even balance the carpet remnant on their head. They roll them up and look through the pieces, like pirates searching for treasure. Regardless, they got their treasure; they received a space to call their own. And all the other children at their seats are now behaving, because they too want to be in a space somewhere in the room they can call their own.

Carpet remnants can be used for small-group show-and-tell. Only the person on the carpet has permission to share an item or ideas; then the carpet is passed on to the next respectful audience member.

Carpet pieces can also be used in cooperative math groups. Items such as marbles or buttons can be put on each remnant as the students learn about addition, subtraction, or fractions.

Carpet remnants are used simply to promote a relaxed atmosphere and to create movement and flow in the room.

Volume Meter

In my first years of teaching, I came across a snippet of an idea in a professional journal. It briefly stated how a teacher made individual volume necklaces for each of her students to help with noise levels in the classroom. Of course, every year I have had an overexcited or loud student, so I naturally connected with that idea. As a first-year teacher, though, I did not have time to create individual items of any sort.

Later, I modified the idea to what would be most helpful for me in my classroom. I decided to introduce my students to a classroom volume meter. I made my volume meter as a simple round clocklike meter from construction paper. It is about ten inches in diameter. I had my assistant stencil the numbers 0 through 10 on the outer edge of the circle. The meter includes an arrow made from construction paper held in the center with a brass fastener.

We practice voice volume tones as a group. The children love to practice a loud "10" voice and a quiet "1" voice. I introduce this skill as a whole-group activity. We carefully practice all the numbers, and I explain to the students that I need them to use certain number voices during the course of the day. For example, when the phone rings in the classroom, I simply say, "Volumes down to zero." All the children drop their voices down to zero. I can hear a pin drop as I answer the phone. When I get off the phone, I say, "Thank you. Volumes can go

Lydia turns the volume meter to 2 as the teacher reminds the boys and girls to look at the volume meter and take note of what number their volume should be set at.

back up to three." The leader of the day turns the arrow so it points toward 3, and the children continue with their work. At certain times throughout the day, I ask any very loud children to look at the volume meter as a reminder to lower their voices.

The volume meter not only gives children the opportunity to move, by twisting their imaginary volume meters or by literally adjusting our classroom volume meter, but it also gives them a visual picture to key into. It also gives them power to control their own volumes. Sometimes, I have children use their imaginations as though they are truly wearing an individual volume meter. This comes in handy in the hallway when the volume meter is left back in the classroom. I simply make a twisty motion in front of my body and instruct, "Volumes turned down to one, please," and the children pretend to twist imaginary volume meters as their voice levels go down.

As a veteran teacher now, I use the volume meter for various activities throughout the day. The leader of the day or the teacher is the only one to turn the volume clock to its appropriate number. For instance, I may announce that I need Emily to turn the volume clock down to 2, and as all the other children notice Emily turning it to 2, they drop their voice levels. The next day, when I have a new leader, I ask that student to turn the volume meter down, and so on until everyone has had a chance to manipulate it. Once again, it is a simple technique to help with classroom management and to promote positive behavior within the classroom.

Helpers: Effective Movement in the Classroom

If students are able to perform a task in the classroom, then you should have them carry out that job. I strongly believe that we need children to be helpers for several reasons. Most importantly, I believe that children who feel needed tend to distance themselves from drugs. While taking classes on the topic of substance abuse and working on my therapy certification, I encountered many workshops involving addictions and addictive behavior, all of which support this idea. Furthermore, getting students active and moving while helping out in the classroom allows them directly to embark on their journey ahead.

When we were an agrarian society, children had almost endless tasks. They were needed on the farm, they were needed for the family to function, and they were needed as helpers in one-room schoolhouses.

In today's society we have begun to cater to children. They now do not have to dress warmly for school because the buses are practically a taxi service, picking children up at their front doors. We are also teaching our children instant gratification. We have such modern conveniences as microwave ovens, dishwashers, cell phones, laptops, and every other doohickey known to us. We no longer have to wait to make a phone call; we do it while eating in a restaurant. Most children do not even know how to pop popcorn the old-fashioned way. Rather it is done within three minutes in the microwave. Families no longer have to work together to wash, dry, and put away the dishes. Instead, you press a button or two and a machine cleans the dishes for you. And information can be obtained within nanoseconds from our computers.

As convenient as all this may sound, it is not healthy for our youngsters. By catering to every whim and instant gratification, we set aside much-needed fundamental values. The message of today's society is that if you buy more and do less, you are successful. This confusing message is leaving our children baffled. Their emotional and occupational selves are bewildered by these illusions.

Basically, today's children do not feel as needed as they once did. The result is that they have a great deal more time for distasteful and offensive television and video games that are full of violence. Children at the earliest of ages are now turning to drugs and alcohol as a coping strategy.

They are screaming for responsibilities and small triumphs that will help them feel truly successful. We as teachers can provide some of this sense in the classroom. My rule of thumb is that if a child can do a task, we should let a child perform it. Children moving as they wash tables together, or pick up scrap paper with one another after an art project, provides not only movement but the sense of a working community. That alone honors our social dimension. Our classrooms are not just *our* rooms, they are the students' rooms as well. By working together cooperatively and taking care of all the tasks that need to be done, we'll form a supportive classroom environment. By doing this, children feel needed, helpful, and appreciated. Furthermore, we are not just teaching the intellectual child, we are teaching the social child about community. We are educating the emotional child about cooperation. We are cultivating the occupational child with task time. By allowing children to take care of such things as cleaning chalkboards and erasers, turning lights on or off, cutting out laminated items, washing tables, organizing the classroom library, and helping with snacktime, we are helping them become respectful and responsible citizens.

When we provide children with many opportunities to take care of the classroom, they gain a sense of ownership and power. They feel it is their classroom. When similar opportunities are given at home, the children will flourish. Of course you may hear grumbling when you ask them to wipe the whiteboard, wash the chalkboard, or organize the book center. Nevertheless, they will feel their sense of worth, feel appreciated and approved of as a result of their gestures of helpfulness.

Quiet Tricks

I once heard a teacher say, "I'd rather have a root canal than walk in the hallway with my kids." She essentially was sharing that her kids are full of energy, movement, and noise, and bursting with it all in the hallway. It is one thing to be in the confines of your own classroom with their energy. In the hallway, however, where everyone has a chance to view your management skills, you need to have some quiet tricks up your sleeve as you get from one end of the building to the other with your twenty-plus students.

Young children seem to be naturally loud. Their spirits are much larger than their small bodies. All teachers know, however, that there are many times when we need children to be quiet for various reasons.

I have been known for having quiet tricks up my sleeve. To tell the truth, there is nothing tricky or magical about using quiet techniques. They are simply another movement strategy, and once again children love to be kinetic, so these ideas are a cinch to employ. Providing simple little quiet movement ideas is another way of helping children move forward.

For instance, perhaps you are doing a theme on snow. Before entering the hallway, when you want the children to be super quiet, ask them to catch imaginary snowflakes on their tongues. Tell them to keep the snowflakes on their tongues until you are done walking in the hallway. Perhaps you are focusing on dental health, so you could ask the children to pretend to brush their teeth and swish water in their mouths. Tell them to keep the water in their mouths until reaching the destination of the gymnasium or cafeteria.

The possibilities are endless. For a "Happy, Healthy Me" theme, ask the children to pop in a bite of an imaginary healthy apple snack. For a winter holiday theme and studying Hanukkah, have the children put in an imaginary bite of potato latke. Ask the children to keep their mouths closed when chewing their food until they get to their destination.

If you are working on a certain letter of the week, such as C/c, have the children use their imaginations to put cantaloupe, crackers, or cookies in their mouths. Later you can graph which C/c foods they put in their mouths when they were walking to music class.

Quiet tricks are a way of connecting the critical attributes of a particular theme to your classroom management and positive discipline style. They are a further way of integrating things. Using quiet tricks in a positive manner is truly a better strategy than using a grouchy negative voice and saying, "Shhh! Stop talking." Students respond better to positive reinforcement and they love to play, so quiet tricks are another positive and creative way of helping children move forward. Furthermore, using these ideas helps children be respectful and responsible, which are moving-forward life skills.

Making Choices

It is important to note the difference between student-initiated choices and teacher-focused activities. A teacher-focused activity is one created by the teacher with one specific objective in mind. A student-initiated choice has a minimum of one objective, but the

Joseph and Haylee look at the center choices and decide where they would like to learn and play today.

teacher allows the student to decide how the objective will be met. The teacher facilitates the learning by permitting the child to honor his or her learning style.

Student-initiated choices instead of a teacher-focused activity help the children retain their learning. The child can choose an activity to be immersed in and still achieve the teacher's learning objective. For example, if a lesson addresses the concept of addition, a teacher-focused activity might be addition problems given from a math book. One activity is given for all the children to complete. Teacher-focused activities do not always take into account the different learning styles of children. Rather, only one learning style is apparent, and it is for the analytical child. Because most children in early primary levels are more movement oriented, student-initiated choices are better to use. A student-initiated choice for the same addition objective would be to provide many activities for children with the different learning styles. One table in the classroom may include math manipulatives for the tactile learners. Another table may include markers, colored pencils, and poster paper for the children who need to see the addition process in a visual manner. In another area, there may be bean-bags and hula hoops for the kinetic learners. And yet another table could include the math problems from the textbook for the children who are analytical.

Once again, by giving children choices, we also give them ownership and power over their own education. This empowerment not only leads the children to retain their newfound learning, it also helps them gain their sense of worth. Furthermore, when a teacher uses more student-initiated choices within the classroom, it creates an enjoyable atmosphere and helps the children realize learning is fun! This is a life skill that will enhance their intellectual dimension as well.

It is important that we keep our children moving forward. Movement invokes growth, and growth is essential for our physical and emotional self as well as for all of the other dimensions of self. Obstacles will be inevitable. It is vital that we teach students that these challenges help us grow, rather than being difficulties to keep us at a standstill. If at any time we detect negativity, we need to do what is necessary to continue on our personal paths in a positive direction. Making progress and getting back on track are vital skills to have in this life. The goal is to move forward toward a balanced life.

8

Provide Empowerment

The mind has exactly the same power as the hands;
not merely to grasp the world, but to change it.
—Colin Wilson, 1931–, English philosopher

Children need to feel powerful. Challenging students especially need to experience a feeling of power. There are two main reasons behind this philosophy of mine. First, there is no question that our youngsters are living in an unbalanced world, in uncertain and irrational times. Our children are subjected to extreme violence; they are exposed to news programs that display dead bodies and bloody information during the supper hour; and they are exposed to raw and vulgar television on a daily basis. It is no wonder our children feel powerless. Second, when there is a large amount of dysfunction in a home, complete powerlessness results. These children have no power or control over their family members' addictions to alcohol, drugs, gambling, or whatever the problem.

One of the missions of today's teacher is to help our youngsters feel a sense of power. Strength enhances all the dimensions of the self. Even children who come from respectable homes at times feel powerless. In their families, they receive the support and guidance they need, but it only takes a few moments away from the sanctuary of the home to feel the chaos and absurdity of an unbalanced world. All youngsters need to feel strong by tapping into the inner knowing of their spirits.

Gaining a deeper understanding of why students misbehave will help you understand the nature of children and parents you consider difficult. Here you will also find activities and ideas to help you, your students, and their parents feel that innate power of the spirit.

Proactive Parent-Teacher Communication

Among the many courses and workshops I've taken through the years, I highly recommend those by Lee Canter, an expert in the field of education and a creator of many books, videos, and courses about succeeding with difficult children. I recall taking a course from him that helped my approach to classroom management. Although it was years ago, some of his strategies have become such a part of me and how I handle situations in today's world that I want to guide anyone in education who is having a difficult time with students to read his work. I would like to dedicate this idea to him, because in his course I listened and learned about connecting with parents. Mr. Canter certainly advocates convincing parents to work with you as an educator. This is how I use his proactive strategy.

Proactive parent-teacher communication is about connecting with parents on a positive note. We as teachers want our demanding student—let's call this student Bryan—to do well in school. Nevertheless, he is constantly misbehaving. He inappropriately touches and pokes his classmates; he fidgets and cannot sit still to hear the instruction; and he impulsively shouts out answers and continually acts up in the classroom. The typical teacher takes time away from Bryan's recess and calls the parents to let them know Bryan has made bad choices at school again. This is a typical cycle throughout Bryan's years in elementary school, and things only get worse as he enters middle school and high school.

Let's take a moment to understand why Bryan is misbehaving. By having a deeper understanding of his circumstances, we will be able to see the situation more clearly and be able to give the appropriate responses and actions Bryan really needs. First, understand that Bryan is not acting up to "get you." He is not acting up to try to make your life miserable. Although you may feel miserable at those difficult moments, the reality is that Bryan's life is miserable. He comes from a dysfunctional home in which his father is an alcoholic and his mother works two jobs to make ends meet. At times, the home has no running water and the electricity has been shut off. Nevertheless, they are able to scrape enough money together for cigarettes and alcohol. While in bed at night, Bryan hears such comments as "Shut up" and "Why are you so stupid?" In his waking hours, he hears "Quit being a crybaby." His family activities are limited, and his basic form of entertainment is the television.

Bryan misbehaves at school because he is craving not only attention but gentle, firm limits as well. He lacks motivation because the work is too hard. The parental support at home is not there. Bryan is left on his own to struggle with reading and homework. The last thing Bryan needs is another phone call from the teacher to say he's not doing well in school. Let's assume Bryan's dad had similar problems in the classroom. His memories of school are not pleasant ones, and the teacher calling to complain about his son will only bring up more negative emotions about school in general.

Although this looks like a vicious circle, you as the teacher have some power to change it and make it better. Let us review what we as teachers truly want. We want Bryan's parents to be more involved with him and his education. We want Bryan to complete his work and follow the basic rules at school. This will not happen by the teacher shaking her finger at Bryan and then shaking her finger at the parents.

The situation could possibly improve, though, by using some proactive approaches.

One way is by calling Bryan's family before the school year begins. Of course when you first call, the parents will be thinking, "Bryan hasn't even started school yet. What's the problem already?" Introduce yourself and explain that you are calling parents to help their children get off to a good start because you truly want them to be successful in school. Ask the parents if there's anything you should know about their child before school starts. Explain that this information will help you in preparing the child for a successful year. Tell them how you look forward to talking with them from time to time to share news about their child.

As the school year begins, work diligently to focus on the other children's good behavior. Bryan, of course, wants to be noticed and will be trying to make good choices. The second you notice his good behavior, point it out. Let him know that you are going to call his parents to let them know how hard he is working at school to make good choices. Follow through. Send notes home about Bryan's good behavior. He will make sure his parents see these letters. His mom will probably even post them on the refrigerator.

Will this approach change Bryan's behavior permanently? Probably not, but it will make life better for him. It will show him the rewards of positive behavior and give him the positive attention and gentle, firm limits he needs. It will also involve his parents in his education on a positive note rather than a negative one. Then when you do have to call his mom or dad about an incident, they may be more likely to hear your concerns.

Proactive parent-teacher communication benefits everyone involved. It is much better for a teacher to construct her energy more positively rather than building up negative energy. This is helpful not only for your emotional dimension but for your physical, spiritual, intellectual, and occupational aspects of self as well. We feel better emotionally when we make someone smile. Our physical body responds to life better when we focus on positive attributes. We feel spiritually uplifted by using kind words and seeing people's good sides. And, of course our intellectual dimension strengthens as we occupy our time using positive thoughts, words, and actions. Bryan benefits because he actually needs some positive attention in his life. And Bryan's parents benefit because they need some positive words and hope sent their way too.

One way to keep track of how you are doing with touching base with parents on a positive note is by journaling throughout the year. I simply jot down the date, time, and whom I called and why. This information is also helpful for next year's teacher. Another way is to simply put the information on a sticky note and place it in a folder with the child's name on it. Little gestures like these have helped me save time and energy, all of which helps us stay balanced in today's world. You will be amazed at how much less energy you use by making these positive contacts.

Role Playing

Children love to role-play, and they are naturals at it. In psychodrama therapy, I learned from my mentor, the late Karen McNamara, ACSW, TEP, of the Finger Lakes Psychodrama Center, originally based in Hammondsport, New York, that the more roles we play in this life, the more our true selves will eventually emerge. I have always found this philosophy very interesting. The more roles we play, the more we emerge. This is what we want to help children accomplish: to help them *emerge*. Contrarily, many youngsters today are finding it easier to *submerge* into drugs, alcohol, premarital sex, eating disorders, and other addictions. Our job teaching students how to emerge into their true self is difficult. Role playing can be a powerful tool that helps children expose their real spirits.

Let's first discuss the essence of the "true" self. The true self is the uniqueness given to each of us. When individuals allow their uniqueness to shine, they are allowing their true selves to emerge. This is also true with spontaneous creativity. When individuals allow their creativity to flow and be spontaneous, they are giving space to their true selves. This is why role playing is so powerful. Role playing is creative and spontaneous—and it permits us to play a role with which we might be uncomfortable. Ironically, by playing a part, a different role than we are used to, we encourage our true self to surface.

Power Roles

Since the dawn of television, there have been personalities and cartoon characters that stay in our minds for a long time. These characters may include Popeye, the Care Bears, the Hulk, the Pokémon crew, Power Rangers, Spiderman, and Batman. Why are these characters so popular? They are admired because of their powers. Yes, even the Care Bears have power. Each of them has a special symbol on its round belly, and each can do things that are unique. Regardless of which newest, got-to-have-it toy craze you mention, the point is that they all hold a magical power for children. Children felt that "power" so strongly and adults wanted to provide it so much that a Cabbage Patch Doll craze and an underground Pokémon buying frenzy developed. Parents would do anything to obtain these icons. All these characters have one thing in common: special power. Everyone wants that external special power a trading card or doll promises to provide. Some people pay ten to fifty times more than the toy is actually worth, and why? They want themselves and their children to have the "power."

Power roles are role-playing activities that help children tap into their innate power. These activities give children an intrinsic sense of power, and in a positive way. It keeps them looking at their own intrinsic power instead of looking for power externally. One example of a power role is the kinetic learning exercise for the creative self in chapter 5, The Creative Dimension: Inventing Your Helpful Person. The original activity about creating a character whom the teacher or class interviews can be turned into a power role by making a few minor changes.

Provide some props, such as old shirts, pants, skirts, shoes, and purses. Furnishing hats, paper, pencils, scarves, and whatever else you can come up with will be helpful. Explain to the children that they will be dressing up to create a character who has special power. They will invent this individual by using the props provided. Each student should give her person a name and identify the character's unique power. After everyone has dressed up, created, and thought about his person, begin an interview process. Draw out from the students what makes their characters unique and what gifts their characters hold. Ask the student questions, making sure the student replies using the pronoun *I*. For example, if you ask the character, "What is your name?" the student should reply in first-person narration, using such words as *my, me, mine,* and *I* when discussing the power role. Some other important questions to ask their power person include, "What is the most important thing about you?" and "Tell us about your power." Keep the questions open-ended. Open-ended questions and statements draw out students' spontaneous creativity and higher levels of thinking.

This particular exercise is also about being naturally spontaneous and trusting what comes up. Once again, interesting and subconscious information will emerge. The teacher's responsibility is to draw out the character's power. The whole objective for this exercise is to help all children find their internal powers. Remember, the more roles we play, the more we emerge. Help the children emerge by asking open-ended questions. For older students, you can also discuss how their power roles relate to them personally. Help them see their connections to the roles by asking the students to write or draw them as they are explaining them.

Villains and Other Character Roles

Children are asked to behave all day at school. They come home and parents want them to be good as well. Children cannot be good all of the time. Behind teachers' backs and on the playgrounds throughout the world, children are trying out being naughty. They actually may know in their hearts that they are not making good choices. And after their wayward behavior has come out, their guilt usually sets in. Why? Because children want to please adults. They want to make good choices. It is in their innate goodness to be seen and heard positively. Realistically, though, children cannot be good all day, all evening, every minute of every hour. They are young human beings learning how to behave. Children need to practice all types of situations, good and bad, to learn what is appropriate—and not appropriate—behavior.

By having students play villain roles and other roles that are not perfectly behaved, children can "be naughty" in an acceptable, creative, and educational way. For example, after reading a particular book that has a villain or a scoundrel character, allow the children to bring in dress-up clothes and props that represent the individual. Divide the students into groups of four or five. Allow all individuals from each group to portray their versions of the villainous character. Initiate an interview process with open-ended questions.

The goal is to let each of the students get into the role. You will notice that several children portray parts of their character's personality more strongly than others. Other children may reveal a different set of the villain's characteristics more powerfully. By letting them become their role, you are giving students the power to develop their creative, emotional, and intellectual dimensions. You are giving them permission and approval to "be mischievous" in front of you. By trying out different roles, students develop appropriate behavior. This is all done in the safety of the classroom setting. Role playing is a powerful tool, not only for literature and other educational purposes, but for empowering our youngsters as well.

To extend the role-playing activity to another level, ask the students how we could rehabilitate the villain or scoundrel.

Mirror/Model Techniques

The mirror technique is a simple method I learned years ago while working in a therapy group with Zerka T. Moreno, the well-known teacher of master-level psychodrama students. At the time of this writing, she is still giving workshops at ninety-one years old. Her husband, J. L. Moreno, twenty-eight years her senior, was the creator of psychodrama therapy. As a teacher, I modified this long-established psychodramatic technique to meet my educational needs. I simply added the modeling part to it and began using it in the classroom to help today's children. As a result, my way of using it may have a distinctive twist from the original mirror technique; nonetheless, it is truly for the educational setting, and its objective involves a procedure you use to elicit good behavior from children in the classroom.

As a side note, adults oftentimes feel the twinge of some small mistake they have made in the course of the day. Perhaps it was an action or your words, or both. When this happens, try practicing the mirror/model technique on yourself as a way of improving this tendency in general. For instance, let's say you off-handedly remark to a colleague in the break room, "Wow! You look tired today!" Almost immediately you notice that your words and tone make your colleague feel bad about herself. Later, when you get a chance, try out the mirror/model technique privately in front of a mirror. Repeat your facial and body gestures and use the same tone while saying, "Wow! You look tired today!" Note how it made your colleague feel. Now "model" other phrases and tones in front of the mirror that may have a more positive tone. For example, say, "Spring break is around the corner. I can't wait to get more sleep." Or, "Hi Beth, how are you doing today?" Having good intentions is a good place to start when becoming balanced in all these areas.

The mirror/model approach allows the children to consciously make better behavior choices. This technique is different from the teacher's telling a student how to behave. The mirror/model approach has the children viewing themselves behaving inappropriately—the mirror part of the technique. Then, the teacher demonstrates the appropriate behavior for the children—the model part of the technique. In other words, the children first see how they inappropriately looked to others and then they view what the appropriate behavior looks like. Lastly, they get to practice this newfound model behavior in the situation in which it was mirrored.

This procedure gives children the power to change their negative behavior to positive conduct. Allowing children to make the behavior change on their own strengthens their emotional, social, and intellectual dimensions. The mirror/model technique does take some practice. Nevertheless, once you feel comfortable with it, you will see why it is a powerful method for both you and your students. Let's first discuss exactly what it means to mirror and model the behavior.

Mirror

To mirror a child, you simply do as the child does. You can even exaggerate the behavior somewhat to make it more dramatic and memorable for the child. This will help the child keep in mind how he looks when acting up. For example, I once had a student who would throw a temper tantrum when it was time to clean up. At almost every transition time, he would throw himself on the carpet and thrash around. To mirror him, I would throw myself on the carpet, too, and yell and pitch a fit just as he was doing. It made all the children, including him, stop what they were doing and look at how inappropriate this type of behavior was. After I mirrored what the student looked liked a few times, he began to choose more appropriate ways to handle his anger.

You need to be careful when exaggerating and being dramatic using this method. The last time I used this mirror technique, I threw my neck out. I actually had to go to the nurse and get an ice pack.

The mirror part of this technique should be used to simply show the child how she looks to others. You can sit beside the child and show precisely how she appears. Begin by saying, "I want to show you what you look like. Please watch me carefully." Often a crying child would watch me and immediately begin to laugh because she had never viewed herself in such a tirade. It is a powerful technique.

You can use the mirror method for other issues, such as whining, disrespect, or lack of motivation. Simply mirror the child's voice and body movements. Show the students what inappropriate behavior looks like. This is why television is extremely popular with youngsters. They often need to see things to understand. It is important when mirroring another individual to reflect that person's words, feelings, body posture, and all movements to leave that memorable impression you are striving for.

As a professional teacher and therapist, and as a parent, I know there are things we sometimes do not want to look at; however, it is important that we do look at them. This is especially true with children. We are trying to raise healthy, happy, and productive members of society. This technique helps in creating that. When my son was very little, he didn't like me to mirror him. I would later explain my reasons to him, when we were away from the mirror moment, during dinner or doing our nighttime ritual of getting ready for bed. I'd say, "I know sometimes you don't like it when I show you what you look like, but I love you, and I want you to grow up to be the wonderful person you are becoming. So my job includes showing you how to make better choices in this world. I'm not picking on you or belittling you, I'm showing you the more appropriate way to act, the big boy way to do it." Explaining your actions in a gentle, caring way is always helpful, and furthermore it helps children feel respected.

Model

It is critical that you also use the model part of this technique. It is even more important that you praise children immediately after they try out the new behavior. Remember, children who are acting out are in most cases seeking attention. If we can give them massive amounts of positive praise and attention for all their efforts, everyone involved will benefit.

The model part is critical because youngsters need to see well-mannered and appropriate behavior. Many children, especially the most challenging ones, do not have many opportunities to see respectable and proper behavior in its correct form. For this reason, we need to model the appropriate conduct, in its finest manner, as often as we can.

As an example, let's say you tell a student, "Samantha, I need you to finish up now," and the child responds in a rude, disrespectful tone, "I aaaaammmmm!" Simply say, "Samantha, I want you to see what that looks and sounds like." Then repeat the command, "Samantha, I need you to finish up now." Step to one side and respond with Samantha's bad-mannered attitude: "I aaaaammmmm!" Afterward, in your teacher role, say, "Now I want you to see the respectful way to answer me." Repeat again: "Samantha, I need you to finish up now." Step to one side and act as Samantha should with a respectful tone: "Okay, Mrs. Fishbaugh!" Wrap up the lesson by telling Samantha you would like for her to try it now using the respectful voice. Repeat the instruction and have Samantha practice the correct behavior. Be sure to praise her for the respectful tone. This reinforces what she has been taught.

After children learn their new appropriate behaviors, give them opportunities to practice. When situations arise (and they will), it usually works to say something like, "Hey, why not try out the new behavior you were practicing yesterday?" This is much better than saying, "Will you stop? I keep telling you not to do that!" Once again, immediately congratulate the student for trying out the new behavior. Praise the child for how grown-up and respectful she sounds.

More Mirror/Model Techniques

I once had a boy, Jason, in my classroom who was labeled autistic. He often would yank toys away from another child. His eyebrows would be furrowed as tightly as possible, and he would have on his full-anger face. Children in my class were scared of Jason. At some point, I decided to carry around a little pocket mirror so he could view his face when these situations occurred.

One day, while playing at the construction center, another boy took a large block to add to his sculpture. Jason put on his angry face, jerked the block away from the boy, and said, "I want that." Right away I pulled out the mirror and said, "Freeze. Look in the mirror. Does your face look polite and happy?" He tried justifying his actions. I said, "No! I want you to watch me." Then I mirrored what he had done, using my exaggerated angry face and voice.

By this time, the whole class had stopped playing at the centers and was more interested in this appropriate-behavior lesson. I asked Jason how my face looked. He told me it looked mad. I told him I was going to show him how to use a polite and happy face. Next, I modeled appropriate behavior. I embellished it by using more pleases and thank-yous and hugs than typical. I said, "Joey, may I please use that block when you are finished? Thank you, Joey, for being so nice." Afterward, I gave Joey a hug. I asked Jason which behavior would be better to use. He, of course, picked the one that was pleasant. I instructed Jason to try out this new behavior. I am always amazed how accurately children get the facial and body mannerisms from the modeling part. Jason looked just like I did. I praised him immediately for using this new behavior, and the rest of the class members went back to their business. Over the next few days, when conflicts arose, I would remind Jason to try out his new behavior.

The mirror/model approach allows children to intrinsically choose appropriate behavior. It is a powerful technique, because it shows children what they look like when they act up. This approach also gives students the opportunity to practice their new behavior on a continual basis. With my little reminders to "try out your new respectful behavior" and "try using kind words," the children will begin to use them. It may take extra time and it sometimes feels like an uphill battle, but it is worth it. It is worth it because the alternative is to ignore bad habits and allow troublesome behavior to become a child's common way of acting. And the unbalanced world would love you to overlook it. Do not let disrespect get by you. Your attention and care with this issue are an awesome gesture in today's teaching world.

• • •

We need to provide children with opportunities to feel positive power. In a world filled with chaos and irrational behavior, it is easy for us to feel powerless. Powerlessness takes away a person's ability to think rationally. When children, or adults for that matter, feel helpless, they often turn to unhealthy choices to take away the negative feelings. This insidious behavior leads to an illusion that power has somehow been restored in their lives. This is how addictions can sometimes begin. And addictions, as we know, take over a person's spirit. Instead, using these proactive activities provides constructive opportunities for people to feel powerful. This type of power inspires and encourages people to live to their full potential. Proactive parent-teacher communication, role playing, and the mirror/model technique give others a chance to gain or regain power in a healthy way. Furthermore, in providing these alternatives, we help balance children's emotional, creative, and intellectual dimensions.

9

Walk along the Path of Justice

*Determination and perseverance move the world; thinking
that others will do it for you is a sure way to fail.*
—Marva Collins, 1936–, American educator, inspirational author

What is important to you? More important, what are you going to
do about it? By standing up for what is right, even in the face of repri-
mand, we strengthen our spiritual and emotional dimensions. I further believe we strengthen every area of our being. Far too often I have
seen fear of speaking, let alone fear of taking action, be a detriment
to the spirit. This is how I felt on that curriculum information night,
when the veteran teacher made disparaging remarks about "loser"
parents. She not only referred to them as "losers" but also said most
of them "do not know anything you are saying" and are "idiots." My
comeback was, "I will try not to remember any of that!" I also "spoke
up" through my posters with "I am here to shine" and other positive
messages. This reinforces the fact that there are always ways to stand
up for what is right in a positive, healthy manner.

Live Past Your Fears

When we know something is wrong, and that issue is important to us, our thoughts, our bodies, and our spirits cry out for us to do something about it. We are now living in a world in which people get away with murder, literally and figuratively. Our society is filled with justifications for every wrong behavior. Too many of us sit back idly and allow unethical things to occur, because we feel it is "none of our business." We do not get involved, because we are fearful of not following the crowd, the majority. Our children not only see this, they feel it. It leaves their emotional and spiritual dimensions hungry for justice and decency. This world is starving for people to stand up for what is right. It needs your support. More important, the world needs you to stand up for what is moral and just. In doing so, our children learn how to take action on issues that are important to them. Teaching children how to be active, rather than passive, helps them build strong emotional and occupational stances. It helps them value life.

When I feel strongly about something, I never sit back, watch it happen, and consider what I should do about it. Rather, I immediately take action. Even as I write this chapter, I am standing up for something I believe in. Although I know I will more than likely be defeated, I am still standing up for the principle of the matter. As the long-standing prayer reads, "Let there be peace, and let it begin with me." Change the word *peace* to *justice* so it can state, "Let there be justice, and let it begin with me." I know the world needs justice, and I believe it needs to start with me. It needs to start with each of us. If we all stood up for what we believed in, we would have strength in numbers. Regardless of the numbers, and regardless of the outcome, our spirits are always strengthened by standing up for what is just.

In my situation, our school budget is being put up for the public to vote on a developmental program that honors children's individual growth and maturation. This program is being cut from our school. The board, the administrators, and the powers that be who run our school are having to choose which programs should be cut. I believe other areas could have been cut more, such as athletics and extracurricular activities, rather than those programs at the foundation of the children's earliest development. I believe it is wrong to cut a program that honors the natural, timely maturation of children. Many people feel it is wrong. But many are choosing not to do much about it except to complain in private with one another. I feel it is more important to take action than to complain. This week alone, I have set up meetings with both the superintendent and the principal. I thought about petitions and other ways to advocate for the program. After my meeting and being informed that the petition would not change the decision, I opted to write a letter stating the program's importance. My emotional and spiritual self would not feel balanced if I chose to do nothing or merely complained. While standing up for something that is important for children, I strengthen those dimensions of myself. I am not knocking or putting down those who did not do anything or simply complained. Rather, I am encouraging them to live past their fears.

Standing Up Using Your Own Unique Style

I, too, know what it is like to be afraid of standing up. Nevertheless, those fears keep you stagnant. By standing up for what is right, you grow. You strengthen your emotional, spiritual, and occupational dimensions. To disagree with your boss is not an easy road to take. In general, standing up is not an easy road. We as teachers do not want to influence our children to take the easy road. We want our children to build values and integrity. We want them to take stands. We do this by modeling it.

I believe we can agreeably disagree. In fact, I think my supervisors have more respect for me, because I am standing up for what I believe in. I hope this knowledge somewhat quells any fears you have of standing up for what is just. We, as a society, need to do more of this in general.

You will not always win when standing up for something you believe in. Nevertheless, you will always enrich your spiritual and emotional dimensions for supporting the issues that are important to you. This is a key aspect to remember when you feel defeated.

When I think of standing up for what is right and taking the path of justice, several colleague friends come to mind. Matt, Patty, and Jon have the ability to address what is important to them, and they each do so in different ways. For instance, Matt has a candor about him. He will address colleagues, administrators, and anyone in the same manner when he feels strongly about an issue. His facial expression matches his statement as he affirms, "Let me be blunt . . ." Patty has a way of bringing her feelings into describing a need for justice. She addresses the same people by beginning with, "You know I felt really hurt when you . . ." and usually ending with, "I think it would be better if . . ." Jon, on the other hand, is a teacher who also holds an administrative credential; therefore, he comes from all angles, not only the teacher's and the administrator's point of view, but more important, from the kid's perspective. He will lay out all the cards on the table, pointing out what is wrong with this hand. He will then provide new cards to show how to improve it. He will explain the problem's root causes, how the issues could get worse, and how to restore the matter by using his plan A, B, or C. All three friends have the courage to stand up, using their own personal styles, even in the face of opposition.

A Case When My Spirit Triumphed

When thinking about the need to stand up, another story comes to mind. Early in my career, I worked for a public relations office. I remember the place feeling like a morgue. The walls were bare ivory under fluorescent lights. Minimal life and laughter went on in the office. Through the thin wall dividers, the only sound you usually heard were keys being tapped on the computers' keyboards.

It concerned me that there was an acceptance regarding this type of atmosphere, so I set up a meeting with my boss to talk about it. During the appointment, I mentioned the need for work to be fun. I told her I believed work would be more productive if there were music, laughter, and little breaks to connect with one another. I shared my ideas of hanging inspirational posters and offering coffee in the morning for the employees in the other offices. We were in public relations, for heaven's sake. She grudgingly allowed me to make these changes. Through word of mouth, I advertised the perked coffee being offered at our office. Within weeks, our office was booming!

As the workload piled up for me, I continually joked out loud that I needed more work. I would shout from my computer over my inbox, "I wish I had more work!" As the keys tapped faster, laughter began to flow through the office. By this time, my boss expected me to stay as late as nine or ten at night to meet deadlines. I even taped to my office door a single-frame cartoon that had the definition of *deadline*. It showed the chalk outline of a body on a sidewalk at a crime scene. Basically, it was implying that deadlines kill. I tried to keep my spirits up. But I carried a workload three people would not have been able to keep up with. I missed my four-year-old son at night. I wanted to be the one to feed him dinner and put him to bed.

I decided to take a stand. I set up a meeting with my boss for the next day. At the appointment, I told her my concerns. I explained about my son and that I wanted to eat dinner with him in the evening. I told her I would be leaving each night at five to go home and have dinner. I compromised, saying that I would return to the office afterward if I had to. In my mind I victoriously thought, "It's about time someone took a stand for motherhood and for all working moms!" I was happy that person was me!

In spite of my inner victory, my boss looked at me and said, and I quote, "I have a dog that needs to be fed and watered as well. You do not see me running home!" She told me I could leave when my work was done. She also began to time each project, making it virtually impossible for me to leave by my five o'clock goal. I gave my two-week notice, left this higher-paying job with its fringe benefits, and took my first private-school teaching job, which involved a $4,000 a year pay cut with health insurance and benefits that I could not afford. My spirit, however, was content. It was content because I took a stand. Although my boss probably felt as though she won in this matter, my spirit had actually triumphed. It triumphed over injustice.

Sometimes Justice Prevails

When I strongly feel a student's needs are not being met in school, I will stand up for the child. And I've found that sometimes when you take a stand, you will win. Justice can prevail. One instance in my teaching career comes to mind.

A little girl in my classroom truly was struggling with the activities the other children were doing more easily. She was having not only academic difficulties but emotional and social problems as well. The special education teacher agreed with this assessment. We worked together with this little girl daily for many weeks, giving a great deal of our energy to her.

After talking with her teacher from the previous year at another school, I learned that their instructional support team, which is usually made up of educational professionals, had wanted her to repeat her grade level there. Her past teacher felt she needed the extra year to gather the skills she had not acquired. The teacher thought that if she did not master these basic skills but went through to another grade level, she would undoubtedly struggle with the entire fundamental skills in that grade as well.

The special education teacher and I agreed the little girl should go back to the previous grade to gain the primary and basic skills she needed. This decision would be best for her development, and we had caught the problem within the first month of school. After several meetings about this child, we eventually sat in on a Committee on

Special Education meeting. During this meeting, two people were disagreeing with our suggestion. They were the people who would most likely determine this girl's placement. The most important thing to note here is that these two people, the ones who disagreed, had never seen, met, or worked with this particular little girl. They did not know her whatsoever. These people were disagreeing with us, even though we were the ones who had worked with this girl, day in and day out.

At this point, I felt very angry. I could not believe life decisions were going to be made about this child by people who had never even met her. Without hesitating, I leaned over the table and looked into the eyes of these people and said, "I work with this little girl every day. We need to do what is developmentally best for her. She needs to feel successful in this school." I cannot recall everything that was said afterward, but I do remember thinking I probably would have stayed at this meeting a long time to fight this fight. It was worth it to me. The special education teacher and I seemed to be the only advocates this girl had. Ultimately, she did go back to her previous grade level and feel the successes she needed to have before she moved on. It was a heartfelt victory for me to stand up and advocate for my student.

Live by the Spirit of the Law

I believe many teachers probably fear standing up because of the nature of rules in schools today. Our schools are becoming a "letter of the law" environment. The spirit of the law is fading away as relaxed administrators and lenient rules retire.

Consider dress codes, for example. They have existed since the miniskirt era of the 1960s. These dress codes are generally meant for children in the upper grades. Basically, spaghetti straps, tops that show belly buttons, short shorts, and micro-miniskirts, along with dog collar necklaces and other extreme fashions, can be somewhat distracting to the educational process. Because rules against them are in the school handbooks, even early primary students are asked to go to the nurse's office to remove their tank tops that have thin straps and replace them with something that fits the handbook's regulations. Obviously, their little shoulders are not a distraction to the teacher or to any of the other school community members. But the letter of the law states that no students should wear these types of tops.

This is just one example. There are hundreds of these rules in school districts today. Somewhere along the line, the spirit of the law has faded into the beautiful sunset. Not only are our leaders bound to keep our schools fixed rigidly, but many teachers also follow only the letter of the law. I believe the uptight atmosphere and inflexible rules need to be more spirit-filled, considered more in the spirit of the law. I am not suggesting schools throw all handbooks and rules out the window. That, of course, would be detrimental to our youngsters. I am merely stating that we need to use our heads and hearts more thoroughly when we enforce these regulations. Of course, we want our schools safe and secure, but we do not need them so rigid that teachers, children, administrators, and community members feel uncomfortable and awkward in them.

Sometimes it appears the world has become so fearful of lawsuits that everyone is tiptoeing around. Schools are checking off each handbook rule as community members enter the building. It is a detriment to our young population to teach them to live solely by the letter of the law. It is damaging to teach them to live so firmly that they can never bend. It is destructive because it is our world that suffers. We should not be teaching our children to live solely by the letter of the law; we should be showing them how to live more with heart. We should be teaching them to trust their instincts and common sense. By suggesting ways to live more with heart, we are teaching our youngsters how to be more balanced, more human, rather than computerized robot-like persons who sputter out inflexible rules.

Standing up for what is ethically right, moral, and just takes courage. It is important that we give our children the encouragement they need to raise their voices and actions to these higher levels. This type of integrity strengthens the spirit. Let us begin by showing integrity ourselves and demonstrating to our children how thoughtfully following the rules is done. Once again, honoring this part of ourselves in a balanced manner is the first way we teach this type of sincerity to children. We need to continue to honor and encourage their young spirits as they stand up. Standing up is a soulful skill that will help them throughout life. Standing up for something you believe in does not always mean you will get your way. Nevertheless, it does mean you will strengthen your spiritual dimension. And speaking up for worthy causes will always support each aspect of your whole self. For those reasons, it is always worth doing!

10

Celebrate!

*Never again clutter your days or nights with so many
menial and unimportant things that you have no time to
accept a real challenge when it comes along. This applies to
play as well as work. A day merely survived is no cause for
celebration. You are not here to fritter away your precious
hours when you have the ability to accomplish so much by
making a slight change in your routine. Leave time, leave
space, to grow. Now. Now! Not tomorrow!*

—Og Mandino, 1923–96, American inspirational author

We have so much to celebrate! Nevertheless, many people choose not
to rejoice in life. Rather, they settle on being victims or complainers.
There are payoffs for choosing these lifestyles. When you are a victim,
there are weekly support groups created just for you. When you are a
complainer, you can usually find a few people who feel sorry for you.
You usually can also conjure up a few friends who would love to join
you in your irritable words.

Furthermore, celebrating is not always regarded in a positive manner. I notice many people's responses when asked how they are doing. I
will hear things like, "Good" or " Can't complain" or "I am tired" and
"Glad it's Friday." It's the exceptional occasion when I hear a celebratory response, for example, "I am fabulous!" or "I could not be better!"

I believe the internal reaction many people have to such a statement is, "Yeah, right!" or "What does he have to feel so fabulous about?" I also believe the most common internal reaction is, "If he only had my life!"

We need to train ourselves to listen to our inner dialogues. We need to teach our youngsters to do it as well. It is important that we learn how to support one another's celebrations. We do this by becoming conscious of our words and thoughts when others are rejoicing. Awareness is a skill that can be used in all areas of life. I am aware, for example, that we as a society need to celebrate more. We need to do this not just in what we do, such as social gatherings and festivities. We need to celebrate in our minds, our thoughts, and the words we use daily. By turning our inner dialogues to a more celebratory channel, rejoicing filters through each dimension of our selves. The whole self is charged with positive energy. When we do this, the world around us is blessed. Our world is hungry for the positive energy you can offer. Furthermore, it is grateful for the smallest gesture you can make in this way. Included in this chapter are ideas to help everyone celebrate more, especially in the day-to-day tasks of life.

Teach Students to Celebrate the Whole Self

Celebrating enhances many of our dimensions. Our spirits naturally love to celebrate. Our emotional selves get to be in the heart of positive feelings. Socially, we get the necessary connecting time. Today's unbalanced world is hungry for more celebrations. Students are motivated by positive reinforcement, positive remarks, positive anything. Celebrating is simply another method for motivating children.

We need to teach our youngsters what it means to celebrate. It is important that we share with them what a celebration looks and sounds like, and how it affects all the senses involved. The whole self in festive freedom is an amazing internal party. By being in the celebratory moment, our physical self savors the balance of good food, quality social time, or singing and dancing. Spiritually, the creative self rejoices in freely expressing itself through positive emotions and sharing. Occupying time in a joyful space enhances the whole self. Think back to a positive festivity you have attended in your life. I am certain you will be able to conjure up a reflective smile about that time. That reflective smile represents the spirit that once felt the "Whole Self" in delight. By simply celebrating in an open manner, you are teaching children how to do it as well. In addition, you are helping balance today's unbalanced world.

Many children come from homes in which a celebration rarely occurs. When these children do see a celebration happen in their homes, it usually involves alcohol and no children's activities. This is why we need to take many opportunities to teach about being festive. We need to create occasions where children can see celebrations that do not necessarily always include drinking. I always like to share about my wedding and how everyone put their glasses in the air to toast with a nonalcoholic sparkling cider.

Teach children about different celebrations. Once again, discuss how all the senses are involved at a celebration. Teach what a celebration might taste like, what it would look and sound like. Include celebrations in your classroom throughout the year. Of course, some traditional celebrations are Fall Festival and Thanksgiving. The winter celebrations include Christmas, Hanukkah, and Kwanzaa, and February brings Valentine's Day. Of course you have all your children's birthdays, the hundredth day of school, Spring Festival, and, let's not forget, the "end of the year" party. Nevertheless, there are many nontraditional celebrations a classroom can have. Celebrating education gives children a wonderful feeling about school. Here are specific ways to celebrate with your students.

Celebrate Subjects

Pick a month to celebrate a different academic subject. For example, if you choose to celebrate math in the month of September, ask the children what an arithmetic party would look and sound like. Let the children pick the day of the party. Beforehand, have the students make number-sentence banners. Possibly there would be math games throughout the room. Gelatin fruit snacks cut out using number cookie cutters are also a fun treat. Everyone could get three-quarters of a cup of lemonade. Let the children do the measuring. Choose to play songs that have numbers in them. Let the children make numbers with pretzels. The ideas are endless. Pick another month and celebrate a different subject. Once again, it is important to get the children celebrating their education. The students work hard daily at school, so teach them to celebrate their accomplishments. Celebrate every subject area. In doing so, you will instill a love of learning in their hearts! Education this way will be fun for everyone.

Celebrate Theme Endings

Just as you celebrate academic subjects, celebrate at the end of each thematic study. For example, if you are studying about plants, have your children choose a day for a plant celebration at the end of your unit. Ask them what a plant party would look, sound, smell, feel, and taste like. I get my best ideas from the children. They will be your number-one resource as you develop such celebrations. Furthermore, such an event will reinforce their prior learning about plants. Possible ideas include decorating with flowers throughout the room, eating veggie and fruit plants for snacktime, and playing pin the roots on the plant. Once again, the choices are endless.

For a region study, perhaps on China, wear cultural clothing, have a Chinese New Year Parade, and later cook Chinese food and invite parents to your party. Enjoying food together and time with one another is a great experience. Celebrations of this nature obviously should include all the critical attributes of the topic.

Not only can you celebrate theme endings and academic subjects, you can celebrate each month, either at its beginning or end. Involve all the characteristics of the particular month. For instance, January might include snow and cold activities, while June would include picnicking and fun water activities, such as water balloon tosses. By concluding a thematic study with a celebration, you teach a child about balancing work and play. You teach children how to celebrate within life.

Ideas for Teachers

As I've stated, celebrating enhances our whole self. Furthermore, in today's unbalanced times, the education system could sure use more balanced teachers with festive, triumphant, and joyful attitudes. Celebrating is purely another way to offer balance to this world.

Get Out of Your Room

I know there is a lot of work to do. I have a lot of work, my colleagues have a lot of work, and all teachers have an enormous amount of work to do. Nevertheless, there needs to be time to connect with one another on a positive note. In chapter 6, I discussed the importance of taking five minutes in the morning to touch base with friends (see page 86). Celebrate with old friends; make new friends. Take time to enjoy yourself, daily! Whether it is first thing in the morning, on one of your breaks, or at the end of the day, take time to connect and celebrate. The reality is that no one knows what tomorrow will bring. Trust me, if you died tomorrow, you would not say, "Boy, am I glad I stayed in my room and did endless amounts of paperwork." Rather, you would rejoice because you took the time to be with friends. Take time each day to get out of your room and celebrate life. Life is a gift; act accordingly. In doing so, you enhance your spiritual, emotional, and social dimensions. You strengthen your whole self.

Pick a Day of the Week to Leave Early

There is a balance between getting out of your room to connect with colleagues and saying to yourself, "I have had enough of my work today; it is time to leave and enjoy my life." By the way, for those of you who do not know this already: You deserve a life! You deserve a life outside school. It is important that you have one, and, moreover, it is important that you dedicate some time to it.

I learned this the hard way. In my first few years of teaching, I recall that everything I said and did had to with my classroom. It was too much. When I went to bed at night, I was still talking about the students, making up lesson plans in my head, and deciding what I should do about some challenging parents. I was not very good for my family. And in reality, I was not in tip-top shape for my students during the day. I was off balance. I was mostly about work.

These days my life is very different. I have a day on which I leave early (at least as early as my contract states I can leave). As I leave the building, I try to emotionally leave the stress of work at school. Which means, I try not to dwell on the negative events that may have occurred at school. Rather, I might share a remarkable thing a child said to me or a funny thing a colleague did that made my day so enjoyable. I am much more balanced in my career this way. These days I try to share more about my dreams and the positive things about my job. I listen to my own children's and family's concerns, dreams, and everything in between. I must add that on my most stressful days, when dealing with a critical issue at school, there are times I do feel the need to talk about it. For the most part, however, focusing on the positive aspects is the healthier, more balanced approach.

In leaving early from work one day each week, I am able to give more to my job. I am able to do this because I have replenished my occupational self by occupying my time in a balanced way. Sometimes when people are so caught up in their work and addictively drawn in, they become entangled in it. When this happens, they lose sight of the big picture. It is critical not only that we take time for ourselves but that we teach our youngsters about this balance as well. We need to teach our youngsters how to celebrate a balanced way of life.

Be Attentive to Your Words

Be very attentive to your words today. When people ask how you are, respond in a celebratory way. When you eat lunch with colleagues, say only kind words. When you are teaching the children you work with, use only positive phrases. Try this for a day. This experiment has never failed me yet. Tuning your inner dialogues and outer words to a more jubilant channel will give you a feeling of joy and contentment. Sometimes we are not very aware of the words we use, nor are we attentive to our inner dialogues. Take one day to turn your awareness to these actions. I guarantee that you will feel better for having used positive words than if you had chosen negative ones. By shifting our words and inner dialogues to a positive tone, we strengthen our emotional and occupational dimensions. Celebrate your positive self.

Host a Staff-Only Party in Your Room

Host a little get-together in your classroom, and then get someone else to host a party in her room. Do this once a month. Make invitations inviting everyone to come celebrate the first 30 days of school, then 60, 90, and so on. Or if you'd rather, celebrate having only 165 more to go, or 130 or 90 more days until summer vacation. Continue celebrating through the end of the year. In today's school system, it is important that we keep morale and spirits up. Children are coming in with more and more severe issues. Teachers are being asked to do an overwhelming amount of work. We as educators need to celebrate all the work we are doing. Collectively, we are accomplishing so much. Let us get together and commune with one another. We need to be humorous together. We need to celebrate together. We need to commemorate the most important job in the world next to parenting—teaching.

• • •

A celebratory attitude is positive energy. Today's world is hungry for it. When you continue to greet life with a celebration in your heart, life will celebrate you. I am celebrating the truth, which is that we are all here to shine our goodness and our creativity on the world. I want to spread the message as much as possible about becoming a balanced person so that everyone takes time to celebrate the unique passions we each have. The world needs your creativity.

Think about that particular statement: "The world needs your creativity." Now imagine what would happen if every teacher told every child this same phrase. If each and every person heard "The world needs my creativity" throughout his school years, then children would internalize approval and acclaim. Everyone would be glowing with his unique creativity, and what a wonderful world it would be. In reality, could this happen? *Yes, absolutely!* It could if you commit to doing so! Make time to celebrate life! Celebrate your uniqueness and the children's differences as well. Take time to be balanced. Seize time to especially learn who you truly are, what your passions are in this life, and what it is you would love to contribute while here. Shine! Shine now! Do it brightly! Teach your children how to do it as well. It is by far the best thing you could ever do for a child. Be a balanced person who continues to shine and celebrate life!

Additional Resources

Ardell, Donald B. *The History and Future of Wellness*. Pleasant Hill, Calif.: Diablo Press, 1984.

Canter, Lee, and Marlene Canter. *Succeeding with Difficult Students: New Strategies for Reaching Your Most Challenging Students*. Bloomington, Ind.: Solution Tree, 2008.

Dunn, Halbert L. *High-Level Wellness*, 7th ed. Arlington, Va.: R.W. Beatty, 1972.

Harris, Rachel, PhD. *20-Minute Retreats*. New York: Henry Holt, 2000.

Hettler, Bill. "Wellness: Encouraging a Lifetime Pursuit of Excellence." *Health Values* 8 (July/August 1984): 13–17.

Kingma, Daphne Rose. *365 Days of Love*. Boston: Conari Press, 1992.

Larsen, Earnie, and Carol Hegarty Larsen. *Days of Healing, Days of Joy*. Center City, Minn.: Hazelden, 1987.

Lerner, Rokelle. *Affirmations for the Inner Child*. Deerfield Beach, Fla.: Health Communications, 1990.

Olivier, Suzannah. *101 Ways to Stress-Free Living*. New York: Michael Friedman; London: Cico Books, 2003.

Smallin, Donna. *Unclutter Your Mind: One-Minute Tips.* North Adams, Mass.: Storey, 2006.

Thornton, Mark. *Meditation in a New York Minute: Super Calm for the Super Busy.* Boulder, Colo.: Sounds True, 2004.

Travis, John W., and Regina Sara Ryan. *The Wellness Workbook,* 2nd ed. Berkeley, Calif.: Ten Speed Press, 1988.

For more information on "The Six Dimensions of Wellness" model visit the National Wellness Institute at www.nationalwellness.org.

You can visit Angela Schmidt Fishbaugh's Web site at www.balanceteacher.net.

About the Author

Angela grew up in the heart of the Finger Lakes region in upstate New York. Her undergraduate work in elementary education was completed at Keuka College, a private liberal arts–based school residing on one of the beautiful Finger Lakes.

Angela's master's thesis was on the topic of art therapy, and her passion during her schooling became environmental art. She completed her master's degree in education at Elmira College, in Elmira, New York. She is a certified art K–12 teacher and an elementary education teacher as well.

Angela has many years of experience in the field of psychodrama, therapeutic role-playing techniques for developing the true self. She is a master-level student of psychodrama and has been a participant in psychodrama training and education classes since the early 1990s. In 2006 she received her certification in experiential therapy. Angela is a certified experiential therapist, CET II, and a member of the American Society of Experiential Therapists (ASET). She has worked with the incarcerated population and various therapy groups. Her mission is to inspire others to honor their gifts.

Angela's educational work has been at the foundation of learning with early primary children. Throughout her career she has taught a variety of programs, including a 3-year-olds program, prekindergarten, developmental kindergarten, kindergarten and prefirst, all of which Angela refers to as "Life 101." It is her aim to inspire those in the educational world. She resides in her country home with her husband, son, and daughter in upstate New York.